MW00805855

A
A
A

The Five Greatest Secrets of Poker and Life

How to Win at Whatever You Do

the
5
GREATEST
SECRETS
OF POKER
AND LIFE
How to win at
whatever you do

Victor Boc

VORCO PUBLISHING
PORTLAND, OREGON
info@vorcopublishing.com

Copyright © 2013 by Victor Boc

All rights reserved. No portion of this book may be reproduced or transmitted, in any form whatsoever, without express written permission from the publisher.

ISBN: 978-0-912937-63-2

The Five Greatest Secrets of Poker and Life
How to Win at Whatever You Do
Victor Boc

Includes bibliographical references and index.

Self-Help, Poker

Amazon Kindle eBook
fivegreatestsecrets.com/ab

fivegreatestsecrets.com
vorcopublishing.com

Published in the United States of America.

This book is dedicated to Tom Engle,
who played the game of life,
smiling.

INTERNET CONTACT

Email — Victor Boc
victorboc@outlook.com

Personal Website — Victor Boc
victorboc.com

Website — This Book
fivegreatestsecrets.com

Amazon Page — Victor Boc
fivegreatestsecrets.com/aa

Amazon Page — This Book
fivegreatestsecrets.com/ab

contents

acknowlegement

The following individuals deserve acknowledgement for having influenced me: Tom Kruman, John Moss, Bobby Baldwin, Doyle Brunson, Seymour Lebowitz, Carl Fox, Cy Kavoosi, Brandy Kaye, Suzie Mansfield, Johnny Chan, Jack Straus, Jody Plotko, Stu Unger, Jean Woodruff, Joe Karbo, Bill Toomey, Gary Lowe, Dave Wallace, Donna Maddux, Margie Montaigne, Shelly King, Terry Knight, Hoolie, Robert Bolen, Larry Fortener, Lee Pete, Tom Clay, Dave Newman, the man with the funny beard and, of course, Lopez.

introduction

Do you want to be a winner? Do you want to conquer all who oppose you? Do you want to triumph at life? Then read on, because that is what I will show you how to do.

I have been playing poker since I was nine years old, and I've learned a few things along the way. I want to tell you what they are.

I boiled them down to five secrets. I call them secrets because almost nobody knows them. I learned them the hard way, but you don't need to; you have the luxury of acquiring them all in one place, right here.

And get this: These secrets, extracted from poker, apply to all areas of your life. These five secrets will transform your experience of this world. With these secrets, you can win at whatever you do.

When I was child, I did many typical things children do. I built a tree house. I played baseball in a vacant field. I hunted frogs in a creek alongside railroad tracks. But my favorite activity of all was to gather the neighborhood kids and play poker on our front porch. Aah, heaven. I loved it. I loved it not only because I took all their nickels and dimes, but because it was a living expression of my admiration for the exquisite game of poker.

Years later, I took up playing professionally. I played in games wherever I found them. I played in taverns, pool halls and gambling parlors. I played in crummy little cardrooms with guys who spoke only Spanish. I played in the World Series of Poker, long before poker became fashionable. And I play today. But you know what? No matter where I play, from casinos in Vegas to websites on the Internet to tournaments across the nation, the essence of the game of poker is always the same. It's raw. It's real. It's beautiful. And it holds the most powerful secrets of the world beneath its humble exterior.

The five secrets in this book will do much more than elevate your poker game. Improving your poker game is the least they will do. These secrets have the power to enhance every aspect of your life, from boardroom to bedroom.

Armed with these secrets, you can obtain whatever you desire, whether it be money, fame, love or anything else. At last, you can create the life you've always wanted. You can start winning, instead of losing. Rejoice, because this book contains the secrets you've been missing.

This book is not primarily about poker. I discuss a few hands here and there, but I do not concentrate on poker complexities. (Plenty of good books are available for that.) You do not need any knowledge of poker to grasp the principles in this book and derive great and lasting benefit.

Here's the deal. If you want to improve your poker game, I have some valuable tips for you. But if you want more than that, if you want to improve your entire life, then I am holding the door wide open for you. Come on in. I've got what you need.

"There are few things so unpardonably neglected in our country as poker. It is enough to make one ashamed of the species." — Mark Twain

POKER (AND LIFE)

Poker is like life. And life is like poker.

I must tell you that not everyone agrees with these statements. For decades, I have been saying that life and poker are much the same, and I have seen people's knee-jerk rejection of the idea. I have seen how defiantly some people resist a pure and simple truth.

But their denial is good. It gives you an advantage. You should be glad most people close themselves to new ideas, because that leaves greater benefit for you—you with an open mind, who choose to learn and prosper.

Recognizing the similarities...

Poker and life are governed by the same universal laws. What this means is profound. It means you can master the game of life by applying the same principles you would apply to master the game of poker. Lucky you.

The ups and downs you experience throughout life are a direct result of the same factors that govern winning and losing in a poker game. By applying the proper strategy, you can win not only at poker, but at everything you do.

I understand why some people feel compelled to dispute these facts. They are uncomfortable with the idea that life, the wonderful adventure we all share here on earth, could somehow be understood from the vantage point of the poker table. They do not want to think that the process of winning and losing in their day-to-day existence could, in any way, be analogous to winning and losing at poker. They have their preconceived notions about poker, and they refuse to consider anything else.

Even though poker is currently experiencing a massive upsurge in popularity and acceptance, some people still view it as disgraceful. They conjure up images of addicted gamblers tied to crime, drugs and prostitution. They are wrong, of course, but that viewpoint persists among the ignorant. People like that do not want to hear anything positive about poker. They see the comparison of poker to life as an insult to life.

The opposite is true. Recognizing the similarities between life and the magnificent game of poker is a fond tribute to life. Rather than resisting this truth, I urge you to embrace it and learn from it. You derive incredible benefit when you understand the principles of poker and apply them to your individual situation.

Let me ask: How are things going for you? Are you successful at your endeavors? Do you find fulfillment in what you do? Are your relationships rewarding and fun? Are your daily experiences free of worry and stress? Are you happy? If your answer to these questions is anything less than an enthusiastic *yes,* you would do well to rethink your strategy for living. Perhaps you could use a new approach to your everyday affairs. After all, those who appreciate life most are those who achieve a measure of success at winning life's challenges.

Making good decisions...

What is life? In one sense, life is a precious gift bestowed upon us by the Creator Almighty. It is the supreme treasure granted to souls incarnate. In another sense, life is the product of a complicated arrangement of carbon-based matter, quantified by the DNA molecule. Life can be viewed different ways. At the least, life is a mystery, a miracle of the highest order.

For the purpose of this book, think of life as a series of decisions. At every turn, you are faced with a decision. You must decide what shirt to wear, what career to pursue, what person to marry, what city to live in, what diet to follow, what movie to see, what music to play, what hairstyle to get, what name to call your child, what doctor to visit, what gym to join, what bank to use, what car to buy and what time to set the alarm for. Decisions are everywhere. Make good decisions, things go well; make bad decisions, your life spirals downward, ending in ruin.

The essential aspect of life I want to focus on in this book is that life is comprised of a constant stream of decisions. Life is many things, but it is undeniably full of decisions. Well, guess what. So is poker. One of the first things people notice when they study the game of poker is this relentless stream of decisions. You no sooner make one gut-wrenching decision when along comes another. And another. And another after that. And each decision is as perplexing as the one before. It is brutal. And so is life. In this regard, poker and life are alike.

Most people find it difficult to make decisions. You probably do, too. You probably wish you could go through life without facing tough decisions. You can't. If you are alive and functioning, you are forced to make decisions. They are part of life, as they are part of poker.

Battling at close range...

Few people grasp the true nature of poker. At its core, poker is *not* a card game. Players use cards, but it is not a game of cards. It is a game of psychology. Poker is a game of reading, analyzing and understanding people. It is a game of posturing, a game of manipulation, a game of interpersonal relationships and a game of supreme, raw competition. Poker is all these things and more. Just like life.

Of course, everyone has experience at life, but not everyone has experience at poker. If you've never played poker, read the next few paragraphs carefully. I will explain the basic nature of the game.

The concept of wagering has been around since the dawn of humankind. One person believes something. Another person believes something contrary. Before finding out who is right, both parties agree to put a stake on the outcome. Each person places a share of money into a common area to be held in trust until a determination is made as to which person is correct. That person is declared the winner, and the winner is awarded the total amount wagered.

Wagers come in all shapes and sizes. One person believes the 49ers will beat the Dolphins by seven points. Another person believes they will not. A wager can be made. One person believes he can run a mile in five minutes. Another person believes he cannot. A wager is possible. One person believes he might be able to pick the correct lottery numbers. The state believes he (and sufficient millions of others) will pick wrongly. A wager is available.

Poker is a game of wagering. Players sit at a table and use cards to determine the rank of their hands. The players make wagers whenever they think they will end up with the best hand or be able to get other players to fold. Players are eager to bet when they believe doing so is to their advantage.

Most hands come and go without players having much opinion about their chances of winning that hand. Often, one player believes he has the best chance of winning, but no other player disagrees strongly enough to challenge that belief with a wager. For that reason, there is little betting during most hands (in a good game).

Often enough, however, two or more players feel strongly about their chances of winning the hand. One player believes, based on available evidence, he will end up with the best hand or be able to get others to fold. Another player disagrees, believing he has a better chance of having the best hand or getting others to fold. When this disagreement occurs, players take turns placing chips into the pot to wager on their chances of winning.

Every poker hand you play consists of receiving cards, followed by a round of betting. Every time it is your turn to act, you are faced with a decision. If no one has bet before you, you may pass or make the first bet. If someone has already bet, you may fold, call or raise. These decisions form the guts of poker. The skill with which you execute these decisions determines whether you win or lose.

There are two types of poker games: limit and no-limit. (Pot-limit is similar to no-limit.) In a limit game, you wager a set amount every bet. In a no-limit game, you are free to wager any amount, up to the amount you have on the table. The style of play in the two games is vastly different. In a limit game, the cards matter more, bluffing is rare and players usually reveal their cards at the end of each hand. In a no-limit game, the cards matter less, bluffing is common and players usually do not reveal their cards at the end of each hand. Most professional players agree that no-limit is the finer game. It is more challenging, and it is a better manifestation of the essential elements of poker. The poker discussions in this book are based on no-limit play.

When I started giving poker lessons in the 1980s, I instructed students in a game called Texas Hold 'em. Back then, few people had heard of this game. One of my early students tells me he remembers learning Hold 'em, but whenever he tried to deal it anywhere, no one wanted to play. Now, it's all the rage. In the words of Doyle Brunson, two-time World Series of Poker champion, "Hold 'em is the Cadillac of poker games." Hold 'em is, by far, the most popular game today among professional players.

In Hold 'em, two cards are dealt face down to each player, followed by a betting round. Then three community cards, called the flop, are dealt face up on the table, followed by another betting round. Then a fourth card, the turn, is dealt face up, followed by a betting round. A final card, the river, is dealt face up, followed by the final betting round. Betting proceeds clockwise, starting to the left of the dealer. Each player uses the five community cards together with his two hole cards to form his best five-card hand.

The diagram on the next page shows a sample Hold 'em hand. Three players are involved in this hand. You have 7♣ and 7♦, which is a pair of sevens. Opponent 1 has J♣ and 9♥, and Opponent 2 has A♠ and Q♠. After the initial betting round, the flop is turned face up on the table. The flop consists of Q♥, 10♠ and 7♠.

After the flop, you have three 7s. Opponent 1 has 9, 10, J, Q, which is a straight draw. Opponent 2 has a pair of queens and a flush draw. So far, you have the best hand. After another betting round, the turn card is flipped over. It is K♠. This gives Opponent 1 a straight and Opponent 2 a flush, the best hand at this point. After another betting round, the river card is turned over. It is 10♦. This card pairs the board with two 10s, giving you a full house with your three 7s. You end up with the best hand. (For poker terminology and rank of hands, see the Appendices at the back of this book.)

Hold 'em is unique among poker games because the community cards make the experience highly interactive. Truly, you are playing *with* the players at your table. Hold 'em, more than any other game, is a battle at close range. Combining no-limit play with Hold 'em, you have the ultimate poker game: no-limit Texas Hold 'em.

You now know enough about poker to easily handle the remainder of this book. I could explain more—about position, betting protocol and structure of blinds, for example—but you know enough for now. In fact, if you fully grasp the content of the previous paragraphs, you know more about the basics of poker than many people who play.

Shooting your way out...

In my opinion, poker is the greatest game ever invented. I have played other games—board games such as chess, go and backgammon; athletic games such as baseball, football and tennis; and free-form games such as twenty-questions, rock-paper-scissors and tag. No other competitive contest comes close to poker. It is unparalleled in every way.

The fundamental concepts are amazingly simple. You take turns betting against opponents, with cards settling the outcome if needed. That's all there is to it. Yet the intricacies of the game are challenging beyond anything that exists in the gaming world. To play well, you need deep intellect, reliable intuition, unfailing resourcefulness, steel nerves and raw courage. And you need the ability to concentrate for extended periods at a level that is nearly inhuman. No other game demands such a combination of skills.

Let me clear up a few common misconceptions. First, poker is not casual. Many people think of poker as a mellow social pastime, where friends sit around drinking, laughing and whooping it up. Some people play that way, but serious players do not. In fact, there is nothing friendly about poker. You can be cordial with others at your table (and you should be), but the game itself is vicious. Played properly, it is a form of warfare. It is an aggressive battle for domination. I think of poker as "violence, without the violence."

A poker face is not the number-one requirement. I cannot tell you how often I hear this misconception. Nearly every time I mention poker to someone whose only exposure to the game is the media, I hear some lame comment like, "Oh, you must have a good poker face." No, a poker face, that steely-eyed gaze, is not the essence of skillful play. True, you do not want to be sending tells to your opponents, but the so-called poker face is misunderstood. The ability to create a poker face does not make you a poker player. Consider this: When you play poker on the Internet, everyone has a poker face.

Cheating is not rampant. The prevalence of cheating is another incorrect impression held by many. In private backroom games, cheating, although rare, is possible. But in modern casino cardrooms, where most of today's professionals play, cheating is virtually nonexistent. If you are hesitant to play poker out of fear of being cheated, you are overreacting. You do not need to be on the lookout for cheaters. Or crime. Or gunplay. No, you do not need to carry a sidearm and shoot your way out of the casino to protect your loot. You've been watching too many movies.

Women can play. The idea that poker is exclusively a man's game is another falsehood. Years ago, well-known poker authors wrote that women do not have the killer instinct necessary to play well. Time has proven that theory wrong. Nowadays, women compete at every level, and plenty of skilled women win in cash games and tournaments. (Note: Although masculine-gender pronouns are used throughout this text, no slight to females is intended; everything in this book applies equally to men and women.)

Poker is not a game of mathematics. In blackjack, for example, you always have one best move at any moment. Your task is to determine what that move is. If your hand consists of 13 and the dealer is showing an ace, then you should hit. That is always true, no matter who is seated at your table or what they are doing. Poker is different. In poker, you must take other players into account. In poker, the mathematically preferable move may not be wise. In fact, it frequently is not. Top caliber players often debate what is the best move in a particular situation. Poker cannot be reduced to mathematics because there are too many human factors.

Poker is a not game of luck. This is perhaps the most common misconception, and it is dead wrong. Luck averages out. Over time, all players receive the same percentage of good hands and bad hands. The difference is what players do with those hands. A good player will maximize the amount won with good hands and minimize the amount lost with bad hands.

The key element that separates winners from losers, over time, is not the cards dealt, but the decisions made by those players. This is a key point to understand, and it represents a truth few people grasp. Skill, not luck, in the context of an extended period of time, determines whether a player ends up a winner or a loser.

Stu Unger, three-time World Series of Poker champion, put it this way: “In cards, the luck always balances out. The good players are going to win. Any player that thinks card playing is a game of luck—I'll show you a fool. That's what the losers always say. The winners don't worry about the short term; we play for the long term.”

Playing the game...

The key to success—in poker and in life—is the ability to make good decisions. With that ability, you will win whatever challenges you face.

Do not lose sight of the fact that in life, as in poker, you are trying to win. Make no mistake about it, life is a game, as poker is a game. It has different rules and different stakes, but it is a game nonetheless. And the principles that apply to poker apply to life.

The philosopher Thomas Szasz says that what people need for happiness and fulfillment is not wealth, comfort or esteem, but a game worth playing. Robert S. DeRopp, in his book *The Master Game,* says, "Seek, above all, a game worth playing. Having found the game, play it with intensity, play as if your life and sanity depended on it. They do." Donald Trump says, "Money was never a big motivation for me, except as a way to keep score. The real excitement is playing the game."

Poker is a game worth playing—and so is life. Both represent a form of competition. In both, the most worthwhile thing you can do is strive to win. Engage with all your heart in the quest for victory.

I know this flies in the face of what a lot of folks preach these days. They contend that life should be based on cooperation, not competition. They say competition is bad, that it fosters a cynical world view. Let me make one thing clear: I do not care what such people say. I am not after approval or political correctness. I am after reality and what works. If you agree with me and you accept, as I do, the intrinsic competitive nature of the universe, then you know my words are true.

I will not spout beneficent platitudes about how we are all in this together, how sharing and cooperation bring happiness and how the world could be a wonderful place if we would just celebrate together and hug each other. That is all well and good, but it does not win poker games. Nor does it win life's battles.

Much of life is competition. Like it or not, that is fact. If you would rather believe that the fairies of the forest will bless you with good fortune for meditating under trees, that is your prerogative. But that is not my experience of what it takes to win. I don't know about you, but I would rather win than lose. If you are with me on that point, then you are going to love the following chapters.

These five secrets are for people who want an edge. If that describes you, then learn the secrets and apply them to your life. Set aside your doubts, and read my words with an open mind. I know I can help you, even if you think you know more about the subject than I do.

"The commonest mistake in history is underestimating your opponent: happens all the time at poker."
— General David Shoup

SECRET
NUMBER ONE

"Determine what they **don't** *want you to do, then do that."*

The information in this chapter could be the most valuable you ever obtain. It is worth more than any price I could put on it. If I were to charge $10,000, you'd be getting an incredible bargain. This secret has the potential to impact every aspect of your life, to improve every experience you have for the remainder of your time on Earth. How much is that worth? Can you put a price on that?

I am handing you, right now, a piece of information that is vitally important to your future. If you learn it and apply it to your life, nothing will be the same for you from this day forth.

You might think I am exaggerating when I make these statements. I am not. I cannot overstate the power and scope of this life-changing secret. I have given exclusive poker lessons where the only thing I've taught is this one secret. It is that good. It is often all that's necessary to convert an average player into a world-class competitor. And you will not get this secret anywhere else. I have read dozens of poker books and discussed strategy with countless professional players, and nowhere have I come across this concept expressed so succinctly.

This secret may appear deceptively simple, but do not be fooled by that. It is the single-most powerful tip that exists. It trumps every bit of advice out there. You should thank the winds of fate that this book made its way into your life. Reading this chapter will be like finding a hidden treasure.

Figuring it out...

Here is the secret: Determine what they *don't* want you to do, then do that. When you face an opponent in a competitive situation, he will always be worried about you doing some particular action. Figure out what that action is. Determine what he does not want you to do. Then do exactly that.

In a poker game, you often find yourself at a point of decision. It is your turn to act and you don't know what to do. Should you call? Should you raise? Should you fold? You study the cards. You retrace the action of the hand. You ponder the chips on the table. Still, you have no clue what is your best move. You analyze the odds. You consider advice from poker books you've read. You look skyward for guidance. Yet you remain baffled. Your actions in situations like this determine your success as a poker player.

Try this. Ask yourself: What does your opponent hope you do not do? What is the one thing he is sitting over there, at this moment, worried you might do? For sure, there exists some such thing he is rooting for you not to do. He is sitting over there thinking, "Please, God, don't let him do that! Please, oh, please, anything but that!" What is that thing? Figure out what that thing is, and you will know for certain what you should do.

The reason this secret is reliable is because the inner desires of your opponent are based on accurate information. He knows his situation. He knows his cards, his monetary considerations, his propensity to fold and his emotional disposition. He does not need to speculate about those things, as you do. He is the person involved, so he knows, firsthand, every relevant aspect of his immediate situation. Therefore, whatever he is thinking is based on factual information from his viewpoint. His thoughts, whatever they are, are rooted in his reality.

Trusting your instinct...

Let me give you an example of this secret in action. I was playing in the World Series of Poker, main event. About fifty players were still in the tournament; I was one of six at our table. George Huber was seated to my left. George was a well-respected player who had already won a World Series event a few years before. Right then, he was low on chips.

A hand came where George and I tangled. I held 6♥ and 5♥, and the flop came K♣, Q♦ and 5♠. I had the low pair on the board. George bet all his chips, and it was my turn to act.

Ordinarily, I should have let go of this hand. The last thing I wanted to do was double him up, and he appeared to have me beat. He was representing at least a pair of queens, which made me a huge underdog. I decided to wait a moment before folding. I stared across the table, watching him closely. And then, suddenly, I got an impression. Somehow, I got the sense that George was worried about me calling. I'm not sure how I picked up this feeling, but the message was clear and unmistakable. George was sitting over there hoping I would not call. So, according to my secret, that was exactly what I should do. I promptly put in chips to match his bet. George had J♦ and 10♣, which meant he was on a draw. The next two cards failed to help him, and I eliminated George from the tournament.

If you don't understand the specifics of this poker hand, don't worry. All you need to know is that I was able to get a clear impression of what my opponent did not want me to do, and sure enough, that was exactly the right thing to do, even though it was contrary to what good reasoning would say. An analysis of the cards on the table, the money in the pot and the action of the hand would suggest I should fold. Every poker book in the world would tell me to fold in that situation, especially in a tournament. Yet I had something better than all that. I had the most important information there could be. I had an indication that George did not want me to stay in the hand. That was all I needed to know.

Your opponent is thinking something. He is not sitting over there blank in the head. He is considering your possible moves, and there is *something* he hopes you do not do. Find out what that is. Study him. Get into his being. Put your psychological whammy on him. Do whatever it takes. This approach is more reliable than trying to figure out if he is bluffing or how he is playing. Go after one piece of information: what he does not want you to do. If you can determine that, you are golden.

And trust your instinct. If you pick up something, heed what you get. Maybe you notice a bead of sweat on his forehead, a vein in his neck or a blink of his eye. Maybe it's the way he is sitting. It could be a cough, a glance, a twitch. More than likely, you have no idea what it is. Your subconscious mind notices something subtle, something subliminal, something nearly imperceptible. You don't need to know the details; if your perception is real, you have what you need.

This approach to decision-making works without fail. It will not let you down. As long as the message you get is accurate, you can be confident you are doing what is best for your situation. When you use this secret, you go directly after the information you need. You don't get sidetracked trying to evaluate a bunch of confusing and irrelevant ideas. You aim at the target, and you hit the bull's-eye.

Remember what I said in the last chapter about decisions? Decisions are everywhere, throughout poker and throughout life. If you're like most people, you are forever trying to weigh various factors to make good decisions. Any help you can get to aid you in that constant struggle is welcome, right? Well, you cannot get better help than this. If you are able to ascertain, directly from your opponent, what he does not want you to do, you have the most valuable assistance you could ever have. Nothing can top it.

Using the power...

On September 11, 2001, the United States of America was attacked by forces of evil. A band of terrorists steered airplanes into the World Trade Center, the Pentagon and a field in Pennsylvania. Thousands died. Following that terrible event, the nation pulled together in a way seldom seen. While most Americans agreed that military action in Afghanistan was the best way to respond to the attack, not everyone saw it that way. Some pacifist groups took to the streets in protest. They did not want America to respond.

At the time, I was hosting a daily radio talk show from the city of Portland, Oregon. In the interest of understanding, I invited some of these activists onto my program. I rarely took guests on the air, but I made an exception. The debate was heated. Interestingly, a number of callers to the show sided with the protesters, saying that a peaceful response was the best way to deal with terrorists.

At one point in the program, I set aside all phone calls and told my audience to listen while I explained something. I used two full segments between commercial breaks to say what I had to say.

I told my listeners that I knew a powerful secret, an analytic tool that serves as a guide to the proper course of action in any competitive situation. I then explained the basics of poker, giving a synopsis of how the game is played. Then I revealed the secret. I said you can always uncover your best move by figuring out the specific action your opponent does not want you to do. I made clear that this secret applies not only to poker, but to every competitive encounter you face, no matter when or where it occurs.

Then I asked: What do you suppose the terrorists do not want us to do? What do you imagine the leaders of al-Qaeda are sitting over in Afghanistan right now hoping we do not do? What is the one thing Osama bin Laden, at this very moment, is rooting for the United States not to do? What do you think that is?

My guests were speechless. I saw their stunned faces. I could almost hear the wheels a-turnin' in their heads as they stared intently across the table.

Sometimes, figuring out the one thing your opponent does not want you to do is difficult. Making that determination is, after all, the crux of this secret. In this case, however, the answer was apparent. The one thing our enemy was undoubtedly most worried about, the one thing they were hoping we would not do, was go after them. They were surely rooting, above all, for America not to take the fight to Afghanistan and hunt them down where they were hiding. So, according to the logic of my secret, that was exactly what we should do.

When my guests finally spoke again, they admitted that perhaps their reasoning was not entirely correct. When was the last time you heard a talk show in which the guests admitted they were wrong? It virtually never happens! Well, it happened that day on my radio program, broadcast from the studios of KPAM 860 AM, in Portland, Oregon. And every caller to my show from that point on agreed that America should respond to the terrorists. That is the power of this secret.

My radio program that day was memorable because it demonstrated the applicability of this secret. Clearly, this secret is more than just a poker strategy.

Years ago, I knew an old man who claimed no one could beat him at the game of checkers. I decided to conduct an experiment. I challenged him to a game, and every time it was my turn to move, I put my finger on each of my pieces, one after another, and acted as if I were studying the board. What I was really doing, however, was watching him intently, studying his reactions. I knew nothing about checkers, and I made no attempt to analyze any of my moves. I based my actions solely on my sense of what he did not want me to do. When I finally removed his last king from the board, he congratulated me as one of the finest players he had ever seen. (He didn't like that my turns took so long, but oh, well.)

I defeated this experienced checkers player without knowing a thing about the game. I did not need to know anything. I had the best information I could have, the knowledge of what he did not want me to do. That was all I needed to know.

The truth is, I found this guy easy to read. He had no clue what I was doing, so he made no attempt to hide his feelings. Had he known, he could have made my task more difficult. Nevertheless, this game of checkers demonstrated the power and reliability of this secret. As for poker, if I could always know what my opponent does not want me to do, I could win without ever looking at my cards.

Of course, determining what your opponent does not want you to do is not always easy. Sometimes you cannot get a good read on him. Sometimes, you are not even sure who your opponent is.

Several years ago, I knew a woman who had a problem with her neighbor's dog. The dog kept coming into her yard. She tried everything to keep the dog away. She yelled at the dog. She chased the dog with a broom. Nothing worked. I pointed out to her that the dog was not her opponent, her neighbor was. I asked her, "What one thing would your neighbor least want you to do?" She considered several possibilities. "Turn him in to the authorities?" she offered. I suggested that maybe there was something he would want even less than that. "Shoot the dog?" she asked, half jokingly. "No," I replied, "that would hurt the dog more than the owner." Besides, if the owner was a real jerk, he might actually enjoy the ensuing confrontation. There had to be something else.

I asked her what she knew about her neighbor. She said, judging from her previous contact with him, he was a control freak. He was always talking about the power he held over his dog and how the dog loved and respected him. "What if," I suggested, "you were to befriend the dog? What if you were to get the dog to like you? Would that bother him?" She thought for a moment and replied, "You know, it just might."

The next day, she put a bowl of dog food by her back door. From then on, every time the dog came into her yard, instead of chasing it away, she welcomed it. She allowed her daughter to make friends with the dog. She even let the dog into her house a few times. The dog loved it.

It didn't take long for her neighbor to come knocking. "Is my pup, Ruby, over here?" he asked. "Oh, yes," the woman replied, "your dog is in our backyard right now playing with my daughter." The guy promptly took the dog home. The next day, he built a new backyard fence. Never again did the dog wander. The problem was solved.

The first step in winning this particular battle was to figure out who the opponent was. It was not the dog, it was the dog's owner. The next step was to determine what one thing that opponent would most dislike. He did not want anyone besides himself getting affection from his dog. Knowing that, the rest was easy. Sometimes, solving problems requires that you get creative. The solution might not be obvious, but this strategy can lead you to an effective plan of action.

First, know who your opponent is. Then determine what he does not want you to do. This can be difficult, but give it your best shot. If, try as you may, you are unable to make that determination, then proceed based on other considerations. But with practice, your skill will improve, and you will become more effective at analyzing the situation.

Put this secret into action now. Use it at every opportunity. Soon, it will become second nature to you. Whenever you find yourself in a competitive situation, start immediately to figure out what your opponent does not want you to do. The act of thinking along these lines will result in you making better decisions in all circumstances. Equipped with this secret, you will be one tough competitor.

Winning more often...

Competitive situations occur in life far more often than you might realize. You encounter competition not only when you sit down with friends and pull out the Monopoly board. Whether you know it or not, you are competing nearly all the time. Do you think about your everyday activities from the standpoint of competition? Probably not. But you should. If you look, you will see that most of what you do takes place within the broad framework of competition.

If you own a business, you are competing with other businesses that target your customers. If you seek a romantic relationship, you are competing with other singles looking for the same thing. If you challenge a traffic ticket, you are competing with the police officer who cited you. Whether you apply for a loan, buy real estate, look for a job, landscape your yard, cook for a dinner party, debate with colleagues, sell on ebay, take your car for a tune-up, dance at a nightclub or climb a mountain, you are competing one way or another. And in every instance where you find yourself in competition, you can use this secret to nail your opponent.

One word of caution: Do not interpret this secret to mean you should go around doing things people do not want you to do. This secret should be aimed only at your adversaries, not your friends or teammates. For example, if you are sawing a piece of lumber and you get the idea that your wife does not want you to cut yourself, do not immediately saw off your hand! This secret is to be used against opponents when you are engaged in competition. If others are fighting alongside you, do not use this secret against them. Cooperate with team members to defeat your common opponent. There are more than enough genuine battles to fight without also creating conflict with people on your side.

Use discernment in applying this secret. Some battles are not worth bothering about, while others are important and well worth winning. Winning a higher percentage of important competitive encounters will make a huge difference in your life.

When you figure all the instances in life where you face a competitor, this secret has far-reaching implications. Say you, right now, lose (or at least do not win) most of your competitive encounters. Turn that around, and imagine that instead, from this day forth, you come out on top in the majority of those encounters. Over the course of a lifetime, or even a few days, that difference adds up and can have an immense positive effect on how your life unfolds.

Every one of your competitive encounters requires that decisions be made. Make good ones, you win. Make bad ones, you lose. The trick is, of course, to make good decisions.

That's where this secret comes in. With this secret, you have a way to guide your decision-making process in every competitive situation. Whereas in the past, you might have fumbled around wondering what to do, you now know a way to reliably determine your best course of action. Isn't that great? You have a powerful tool to lead you to victory.

"If you know poker, you know people,
and if you know people, you got the
whole world lined up in your sights."
— Bret Maverick

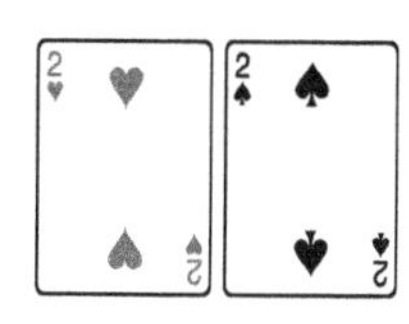

SECRET NUMBER TWO

"Look outward."

Salinas, California, years ago, was a city in transition. The sleepy farming community of Steinbeck's day was on its way to becoming a modern urban center. But you would never know that to look at downtown. Dilapidated pawnshops and grungy cardrooms were the mainstay back then. I know. I was there.

I was fresh out of school, nearly broke and living in downtown Salinas when I decided to take the plunge and become a professional poker player. I needed to start playing regularly, and what better place to begin than a go-for-bust town like Salinas.

The Rex. I don't know why, but for some reason, that was my favorite of the cardrooms. It was a dump like all the rest, but I did well there. Sometimes I won and sometimes I lost, but overall, I managed to win enough to pay rent and eat egg sandwiches.

Over time, I became aware of one particular guy who played there. He spent almost as much time at the Rex as I did. They called him Lopez. Lopez was the only player who seemed to win more money than me. Many days, I would grind out a small profit, but Lopez would rake it in.

I noticed something about Lopez. Every time I looked at him, he was already looking at me. It was uncanny and a bit unnerving. Whenever I glanced his way, his eyeballs were staring back at me. At first, I didn't think much of this, but after a while, I became intrigued. I made a study of Lopez. I wanted to know what made this guy a good poker player, what caused him to win more than I did. Then I figured it out. He was always looking outward.

Paying attention...

The secret is to look outward. What I mean by that is to focus on the people and events around you. Attune your consciousness to that which is happening outside yourself. Set aside your own thoughts and feelings, and aim your attention at the external world, that which is happening around you. Quit thinking about yourself.

I have noticed a correlation. Invariably, those players who consistently win at poker are those who watch others like hawks. They are the players who are always looking around the table, studying everyone, paying attention to everything.

That does not describe the average poker player. Ninety-nine percent of people who play are always thinking about themselves. They are pondering their cards, their money, their position in the hand. They are thinking about their choices and their dilemmas. They have a thousand contemplations, and every one concerns themselves.

How should I play these cards? Am I playing well? Am I likely to win at this table? What kind of cards am I getting? How did I lose that last hand? How can I play better? How is my money holding up? Should I cash out? Should I set a limit? How do I look to the other players? How can I impress them? These are the thoughts that fill the mind of the average poker player. It's all me, me, me.

The average player thinks about things from his own perspective. He will base his decisions on the strength of his hand, the money he put in the pot, his supply of chips, how much he has won or lost and the advice he read in that poker book last night. Again, it's all me, me, me.

That is not the way to approach the game of poker. Even the most well-reasoned thinking along those lines is destined to fail. You may be thinking smartly and accurately, but if your thinking is directed inward, it is no good. If you are thinking only about yourself and your situation, you will come up short.

Forget about yourself. You do not exist. Focus on the other players in the game. Look around the table. Pay attention to everyone. Notice everything. Observe the behavior of every player at your table. Be aware of every action (and inaction) occurring at every moment. Even when you are not in a hand, watch anyway. Always. Constantly. Intently.

You do not need to consciously interpret what you are seeing. You do not need to figure out what any of it means. Just watch. Your subconscious mind will know how to interpret what you see. Even if you think this is not helping, do it anyway. You are going to be sitting there spending time, right? You may as well be paying attention. There will be plenty of time later to contemplate how you performed and what sort of player you are. For now, think only of the other players. Put yourself out there with them. Be them. Think their thoughts. Their thoughts matter; your thoughts do not. What they are thinking is valuable to you; what you are thinking is old news.

Don't pore over your cards. Don't study your chips. Don't regurgitate all the poker advice you've gotten over the years. Get all that garbage out of your mind. Don't play the cards; play the players!

I could have called this secret, "Pay attention to others," but I want to draw a contrast to thinking about yourself. When you are thinking about yourself, you are looking inward. Do the opposite. Look outward.

Doing this does not require that you change your style of social interaction at the table. Be as talkative or as quiet as you like, but all the while, be paying attention. Make this your little secret. I do call it a secret, you know.

You may need discipline to pay attention, but I assure you, if you make it a habit, it will pay off big. Gradually, your game will improve. In time, you will be playing better and pocketing more cash. What's funny is, you may not know why. You may not detect any difference in your playing style. Your success may be a mystery to you. That's how this secret works.

Very few people, it seems, will tell you this secret. Occasionally, a poker book will suggest that you "observe other players at your table." But that is not enough. I am telling you to lose yourself and devote your full consciousness to the other players. Give them your unwavering focus the entire time. Nothing less.

Jamie Gold won the main event at the 2006 World Series of Poker in Las Vegas. And he didn't just win the event, he destroyed his opponents all the way through the entire two-week ordeal. Seldom has any one player so dominated a poker tournament, as Jamie Gold did during that particular World Championship.

Immediately after his victory, he was asked how he did it. What was his secret? What was the biggest factor in his amazing performance? Here is his answer: "I'm playing against the other players, while they are trying to play their cards. I sit down at every table with the same strategy. I want to find out how they're playing, and then I want to figure out how to beat them—whereas they're just trying to figure out how to get the best cards and get their money in there. So, sooner or later, I seem to be able to trick them into giving me all their money."

As Jamie answers this question, what do you hear in his words? I'll tell you what I hear: He was looking outward! He was paying attention to the other players, while they were thinking about themselves. Simple. Yet nothing could be more powerful than this strategy.

Jamie did a lot of talking during the tournament. Everyone remarked how much he interacted with other players at the table. But all the while he was talking, he was intently watching. Talking was his style; looking outward was his strategy.

You know something else? When you pay attention at the poker table, you meet the most amazing people. In Riddle, Oregon, I met a man who lost his leg in World War II. In Gardena, California, I met a man who was sold into slavery in Africa. In Ft. Collins, Colorado, I met a man whose six-year-old daughter died of leukemia. In Buffalo, New York, I met a woman who rescued a drowning boy from a Holiday Inn swimming pool. In Berea, Ohio, I met a man who played guitar with Paul McCartney. In Orlando, Florida, I met a woman who trained astronauts at NASA. In San Jose,

California, I met a man who donated $7 million to Live Aid. In Flagstaff, Arizona, I met a woman who owned a chain of casinos in the Philippines. In New Orleans, Louisiana, I met a man who was shot three times in a drive-by shooting. In Vancouver, Washington, I met a man who was friends with George W. Bush. In South Lake Tahoe, Nevada, I met a couple who scaled Mt. Everest together and survived an avalanche. In Battle Ground, Washington, I met a man who was in the twin towers on 9/11. In Portland, Oregon, I met a man who was among the last troop convoy to leave Iraq when the war ended. I could go on and on.

Of course, meeting people is not your goal in poker. I understand that. But when you meet interesting people (and learn from them) on your way to victory, you are making the most of your experience.

Striking a bell...

Can this secret be used away from the poker table? Does it apply to life? You bet it does! In fact, that is where this secret really shines. That is where its magic will blow you away.

Scientists say human beings are social animals. They say that when people are deprived of interpersonal contact, they fail to develop emotionally and, sooner or later, lose the ability to function altogether. What this means is simple: People depend on other people.

You are no different. You must interact with others as you attract sustenance and good fortune into your life. This is an inescapable fact. If you think you are so high and mighty, so masterful and self-sufficient, then think about this: Every material thing that comes into your life comes to you by way of other people.

The food you eat—you did not grow that food. The clothes you wear—you did not design those clothes. The roads you drive—you did not pour cement for those roads. The building where you work, the park where you play, the electrical grid from which you get power—you did not create those things. Other people did. The gas in your car, the heat in your home and the water in your sink all made their way into your world through the efforts of other people. Even the money you stash in your investment account was transferred to you by other people.

If you give something in return for what you acquire, that does not negate the fact that you depend on others all the way through the process of obtaining goods and services. You are, as we all are, dependent on others for your continued earthly existence.

Because everything comes to you, ultimately, from other people, the actions of other people are important. If you are to receive something of value, it must come, one way or another, through the consent of others. To apply this secret to your life, pay attention to other people. Stay focused on those around you.

Of course, most people do not do that. Most people think primarily of themselves all the time. They make exceptions for family and a few friends, but they give barely a passing consideration to everyone else. These same people struggle through life, wondering why they fail to achieve success. They forget that success in the competitive arena of the world is a joint effort, a result of their individual energy outlay in conjunction with the will of other people.

Stop thinking only about your wants and your problems all the time. Notice those around you. Put yourself in their shoes. Think as they think. Feel as they feel. Pay attention! That is what a good salesperson does.

The first and most important rule of good salesmanship is to *sell benefit.* Explain to your customer how the item will benefit *him.* Do not tell him you need the sale to hit your quota and you need the commission to get a new couch and he should buy this doodad to make you happy. He does not care about that. Nobody does. Except you.

Instead, put yourself in his place and think and feel as he does. Effective salespeople relate to their customer in an attentive way. They forget themselves. They concentrate on the other person.

By paying attention to others, you learn their desires and motivations. You understand what might prompt them to do what you want. The best way to facilitate having good things happen to you is to engage other people, to tap their energies. Other people, taken as a whole, have influence over the events in your life.

I realize this advice runs counter to conventional wisdom. Popular books and seminars preach that the way to improve your life is to get in touch with your inner self. They say you should discover who you are and then work on your deep problems.

That's fine. Inner work has its place. But it is no good at all when you are seated at a poker table. There is a place for resolving inner conflicts, but a poker game is not such a place. Likewise, when you are engaged in life's battles, inner reflection is exactly the wrong thing to be doing. You should be doing the opposite. You should be looking outward.

Self-improvement workshops teach you to look inward, claiming that self-reflection leads to peace of mind. Again, that is true. But you should practice your self-improvement techniques during downtime, not when you are facing an adversary. Competition is the wrong time to focus exclusively on yourself.

Competition is the time to acquire knowledge of your opponent, and the way to do that is to look outside yourself. These days, with everyone preaching the value of looking inward, I want to offer a little balance. Allow me to strike a bell for the wisdom of looking outward.

Aiming for success...

Several years ago, I decided to try my hand as deejay/manager of a new nightclub in Eugene, Oregon. I poured my heart and soul into setting the place up the way I thought it should be. I built a disc-jockey booth and sound system second to none. I designed the lights and programmed the music to make the club a happening place. Everything was perfect, or so I thought. Opening day came—and it was a disaster. Everyone who walked through the door turned around and left.

Four months went by, and nothing changed. In my opinion, our club had the best music, the best lights, the best dance floor, the best drinks and the best staff—yet nobody wanted to be there. We became known as a place that was always empty. To make matters worse, we were losing money, and losing it fast.

Do you know what was wrong? The whole time, I had been focusing on what *I* wanted, on my fantasy of what the place should be. All my efforts were oriented around my own personal opinions and desires.

When I realized this, I removed myself from the equation. I hired a woman to do a survey, and she talked to every person who came through our door. She surveyed patrons at other clubs throughout the area, too. She found out what *they* wanted. She even asked about club names, and I changed our name to "Scandals."

Using what I learned from that survey, I redid everything. The music, the lighting, the sound, the drinks, the layout, I changed it all. Most importantly, I changed my vision of myself within the club. I was no longer important, no longer the star. I did not matter. The customers mattered. They were the stars.

Within weeks, the place caught on. Every night, we had a line of patrons waiting to get in. On weekends, the line stretched across our parking lot. We often reached capacity by 8:30 PM, which was unheard of in the nightclub business. Scandals became the most successful nightspot in the state of Oregon, and it remained so until I departed three years later. The secret to success was paying attention to others. Let me repeat that: The secret to *my* success was paying attention to *others*.

Life is about other people. The happiest individuals are those who devote their life's energy to the call of others. That is why a life containing an element of service, of giving freely to those in need, proves so rewarding. I am not suggesting you devote your life to the service of others. I am suggesting only that you notice those around you.

Imagine, for a moment, you are playing football. You are running with the ball, and an opposing player is planted directly in front of you. You want to get past him. What should you do? Should you intellectualize about your abilities and how to use them? Should you contemplate your training techniques and all the nifty moves you know? Should you analyze the fact that everyone is watching you and what a great opportunity this is to impress them? No, your best course of action is to focus entirely on that player. Forget about yourself, and concentrate on him. Watch him intently. Coaches say you should focus on a point at the center of his waist and nothing else. In other words, get outside yourself.

Say you are placing a bid on a house. What should you do? Should you think about your needs and how much you want the house? Should you bring your own thoughts and emotions into your analysis? Should you base your bid entirely on your situation? No, if you're smart, you will focus on the seller and his agent. What are their motivations? What are they interested in? How might you relate with them to get what you want? You will do best if you concentrate on them, not yourself.

Say you are writing a letter to the editor of your local newspaper and you want the paper to print it. What should you do? Should you focus on the importance of what you have to say and how great you are for writing it? Should you tell the editors how badly you need your letter published? Should you be thinking about all the praise and notoriety you will get once it is published? No, that will not persuade them. If you are smart, you will consider their point of view. What do they want? What is in their minds? What would motivate them to select your letter? You have a better chance of seeing your words in print if you concentrate on them instead of yourself.

Lopez understood an important fact of life as he sat at that poker table in Salinas many years ago. He realized that the secret to his success lay in his ability to tap into others. Lopez was a wise man. (By the way, years later, I learned that Lopez had moved to Los Angeles. The story was that he had earned enough money playing poker to send his son to Stanford.)

This secret works in life, as it does in poker, when you pay keen and constant attention to others. I realize that thinking about yourself is more habitual. It is the easy thing, the typical thing everyone does. Thinking about others is rare among people. But so is success.

You might find it hard to aim for success, but as Tom Hanks said in the movie *A League of Their Own,* "It's supposed to be hard. If it wasn't hard, everyone would do it. The hard is what makes it great."

> "The main skill successful people possess is the ability to closely estimate their chances in life."
> — Mike Caro

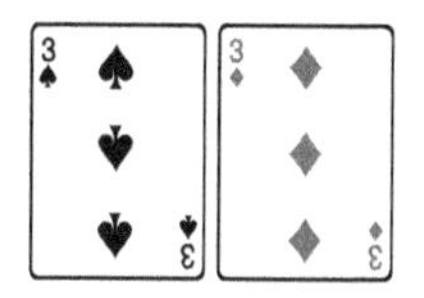

SECRET
NUMBER THREE

"Know your odds of risk versus benefit."

The 2006 World Series of Poker in Las Vegas was a massive event. More than 8,700 players from around the world paid $10,000 each to compete in the main tournament. And the media were everywhere. The place was crawling with reporters running around getting in everyone's way asking dumb questions.

They kept asking one question in particular. Every time they interviewed a player still in the tournament, they would ask, "If I gave you second place right now, would you take it?" Maybe someone had passed around a list of recommended questions and that was at the top of the page. I guess they thought it was a great question. Maybe they thought it was clever. In fact, it was an idiotic question that showed ignorance on the part of the questioner.

Every player I saw who answered that question answered "yes." And the reporter was always surprised by the answer, sometimes repeating the question as if the player must have misunderstood what was asked. Media folks obviously have no feel for poker. A good poker player would never answer that question "no." If he knew anything about odds, his answer would need to be "yes."

Journalists are accustomed to interviewing a certain type of individual. They expect a poker player to behave like a sports figure or political operative, someone who might feel the need to display fake confidence to impress the audience with a positive attitude. "No way, man, I won't accept second place because I plan to win the whole thing, ha, ha." But poker players are not like that. Poker players are: 1) smart, and 2) realistic.

Here is an example of what I'm talking about. On July 11th, the third day of the main event, Greg Raymer, the winner from the previous year, was asked that question as he sat at his table. He had $340,000 in front of him, and he was one of 560 players remaining in the tournament. Here are the exact words he was asked: "Right now, if we offered you second place, which is like four million dollars, would you take it?" Raymer's answer was an immediate and resounding "yes." He added, "That's a $3.65 million overlay. I'm taking it."

Raymer was smart. He looked at his odds of risk versus benefit and knew the correct answer. The only way accepting second place would be a bad decision was if he would otherwise win first place. At that moment, his chance of ending the tournament in first place was a huge long-shot, and someone was offering him second place and four million dollars. The correct answer was obvious. By the way, Raymer eventually got knocked out in twenty-fifth place that year (earning $304,680), so he would, indeed, have been wise to accept a second-place finish.

A good poker player knows how to evaluate odds and weigh them against risk versus benefit. A good player is always thinking that way.

Evaluating your chances...

Let me explain the concept of "pot odds." Whenever you face the prospect of betting, you can calculate the odds the pot is paying you on your bet. For example, if there is $10,000 in the pot, and you are considering the possibility of betting $1,000, your pot odds at that moment are exactly 10 to 1. Since you are putting up $1,000 for the chance to win $10,000, the pot is paying you ten times your bet.

The most basic skill in poker is comparing your pot odds to your odds of winning the hand. Let's say the pot is paying you $10,000 to $1,000 (10 to 1) and your chance of winning the hand is 20% (4 to 1 against you). In this case, you have a good bet.

The reason is because the pot is paying you at a higher ratio than your likelihood of winning. If you made this bet a thousand times, you would come out ahead. You would lose 80% of the time, losing $1,000 each of those times, and you would win 20% of the time, winning $10,000 each of those times. Add up these totals. If you placed one thousand of these bets, identical every time you bet, you would expect to end up with a profit of $1,200,000. That is why this is a favorable bet.

If your pot odds are paying you at a higher ratio than your chance of winning, you have a good bet. If your pot odds are paying you at a lower ratio than your chance of winning, you have a bad bet.

Here is another way to evaluate this. Figure out your chance of winning the hand expressed as a percentage, then compute the percentage of your bet divided by the pot. If your chance of winning is less than your bet/pot percentage, then the bet is a losing proposition. If your chance of winning is higher than your bet/pot percentage, then the bet will pay off in the long run.

To illustrate this concept, here is a hypothetical poker hand. You hold A♠ and 2♠, and the flop comes with two spades and no pairs. You have a flush draw.

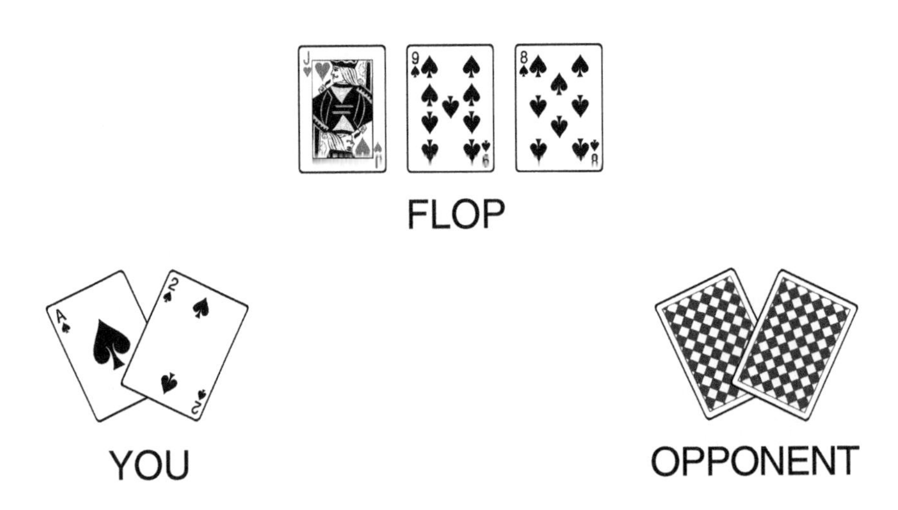

Your opponent bets $1,000 into you, bringing the pot to $5,000. In this situation, if you make your flush, you will likely win the hand. (You could also pair your ace.) The chance of hitting your flush with two cards yet to come is 35% (about 2 to 1 against), and the pot is paying you 5 to 1 on your bet. So, calling (or raising) this bet is a good move. If instead, there were only $1,500 in the pot, then calling a $1,000 bet would be a bad move. That is because the pot is paying you at only 1.5 to 1, which is not a sufficient ratio to justify a 35% shot at winning.

You should also consider your "implied odds." In the example above, with two betting rounds to go, the pot might grow larger. So, if you make your flush, you would win more money than the amount already in the pot. Your implied odds are greater than the current ratio, which means your implied odds argue more strongly for a call (or a raise) of the $1,000 that was bet.

If this is too mathematical for you, don't worry, you do not need to understand the calculations. You need only to grasp the concept of evaluating your chance of winning as compared to what you might lose and what you might gain. Take your likelihood of a positive outcome and weigh that against your risk versus benefit.

The law of averages will hold up over time. The more bets you make, the more your long-term results will agree with what you expect statistically. Flip a coin four times. You might not get two heads and two tails. You could get three heads and one tails, or zero heads and four tails, or some other combination. But flip a coin a thousand times, and you will get very close to 50% heads and 50% tails. It is spooky how this happens, but it does happen. You can count on it. You can *bet* on it. In fact, you are wise to bet on it.

When dealing with probabilities, you want a large number of trials. If you make only one bet, anything can happen. But if you make a lot of bets, your results will align with what the law of averages predicts.

The theory behind successful poker play, therefore, is to make a lot of good bets. Your goal is to, over time, make a large number (perhaps thousands or hundreds of thousands) of favorable bets. If you can accomplish that, you will come out ahead. There are many other considerations in poker, but this fundamental concept forms the basis of sound play. Make certain you grasp this concept.

Many poker players do not understand this principle. I see players all the time who repeatedly place bets that make no sense from the standpoint of probability. It is okay to do that on occasion, but to do it consistently, with no awareness of pot odds, is certain to produce a miserable player grumbling about bad luck. I cannot imagine what is in some people's minds when they make decisions at the poker table. They appear to decide their actions based on whim, rather than anything reasonable. As fundamental as this concept is, few are familiar with it. I have no qualms about calling it a secret.

Here is the best way to implement this secret at the poker table. First, evaluate your chance of winning the hand and weigh that against your pot odds. Determine your best move on that basis. Then take everything else into consideration. Consider tells, bluffs, playing styles and whatever else is relevant. Then decide what to do. You may decide to act contrary to your analysis of odds, but you should start from that point of reference. Always begin by knowing your odds.

Making good bets...

Now, let's talk about life. As in poker, your goal is to go through life making good bets. In life, most of your wagers do not concern money, but they are wagers nonetheless.

Life is a gamble. Uncertainty is an inherent quality of the universe. Therefore, everything you do, every decision you make, can be viewed as taking a risk, placing a wager. Crossing the street is a gamble. You might get hit by a truck. What you normally do before crossing is consider your likelihood of making it to the other side. You look both ways to gather information. You notice that all vehicles are stopped and the traffic light is in your favor, so you figure that your chance of getting run over is small. You accept the risk and go for it.

You gamble when you drive your car. Will you make it safely to your destination or will some crazy drunk smash into you? You gamble when you buy an avocado. Will it taste good or will it be rotten inside? You gamble when you ask someone to marry you. Will you live in peace and harmony or will your mate turn out to be a demon from hell? Just getting up in the morning is a gamble. There is no telling what horrible disasters might befall you before the day is over and you are once again safe in bed. You are gambling all the time, whether you realize it or not.

I laugh when I hear self-righteous politicians debate whether to allow gambling—as if they could prevent it! They are speaking of things like lottery cards and keno games. They must believe that gambling can be restricted to such activities. They must believe they have the power to regulate risk-taking. What fools they are. They don't know it, but everything people do is gambling, and lawmakers are powerless to stop it.

Not only that, but those who know how to gamble are those who will prosper. Those who understand the principles of odds and risk-taking are those who will succeed at the game of life. Instead of pooh-poohing the concept of gambling, we should teach it in our schools! (Yeah, fat chance.) Like it or not, gambling is everywhere. The wise person learns how to win at it.

In life as in poker, your best approach to making good decisions is to first consider your odds of risk versus benefit. Although in life, you are not using numerical calculations, the same principles apply.

Let's say you are considering asking Sarah for a date. She doesn't know you exist. You, on the other hand, worship her with every breath you take. So, from your point of view, a date is in order. First, estimate the likelihood of her saying yes. Then consider the risk versus benefit. If she says no, you will need to deal with the pain of rejection. How badly will that affect you? Can you handle it? But if she says yes, you will get to be with her on a date. There is even an outside chance the two of you will fall in love and get married. Who knows? Because that is certainly a possibility, however remote, it needs to be considered as a potential benefit. Put all the factors together, and make a decision. If the chance of her saying yes is minuscule and the pain of rejection would be severe, you may decide not to ask her. If, however, there is a slight chance she will say yes, and the benefit could be a lifetime (or at least one night) of heaven on earth, then you should work up the nerve to toss her the question.

Let's say you are considering whether to quit your job and start your own business. You have always wanted a business of your own, and right now the time seems right. First, estimate your likelihood of success. Read about businesses like yours and study relevant information. Then consider the risk versus benefit. If you fail, what will that mean to you and your family? How great will the suffering be? Will you be okay? If you succeed, how great will the reward be? How much income might you earn? How much work are you assuming? How much happier will you be? Put everything together, and make a decision. If the odds of success are remote and failure would be devastating, you should probably not take the leap. If, however, the odds of success are reasonable and the potential benefits are attractive and far-reaching, then you should work up the courage to try.

Let's say you are considering whether to take your family on vacation to Disney World. They deserve it, and so do you. First, estimate the likelihood that the trip will turn out well. Then consider the risk versus benefit. How much will the whole thing cost? How miserable will everyone be if the trip goes badly? How much fun will everyone have if it goes well? Put all your considerations together, and make a decision. If the chance of anyone enjoying themselves is slim and spending the time and money would hurt, then you should probably stay home. If, however, the chance of a successful tip is within reason and the excursion could be an opportunity for everyone to have a wonderful time together as a family, then you should go.

I am not suggesting you turn every minor decision into some big, complicated ordeal. Heavens, no. Just take a look at your odds and weigh them against your risk versus benefit. You can do this quickly in your head. Do not labor over precise calculations; keep the process simple. Use this secret as a fast, easy way to approach your decisions.

Many people already have a vague concept of risk versus benefit. Business schools teach a similar approach to investing. But what makes this a secret, and a powerful secret at that, is the idea of using it in your daily life. If you apply this secret to your everyday thinking, you will reap rewards in ways you hardly imagine.

Considering the outcome...

Let me tell you about something I did that most people would say was stupid. I was playing poker in Las Vegas, and this particular trip was proving to be more profitable than most. Meanwhile, every Friday evening, back in Santa Cruz, California, a poker game took place in a room behind a tavern.

I played in that game often. As I sat in Las Vegas playing poker, I realized it was Friday night and the game in Santa Cruz was taking place at that exact moment. I got up. I phoned the manager of the Santa Cruz club. I asked him how many players were seated at his table at that instant. He said seven. I told him to, right then, give every one of those players an extra $1,000 in chips, and I would cover the cost when I got back in town.

Most people would think I was off my rocker to do this. I gave away $7,000 for nothing. What possible logic could there be in that?

Here is what happened. Word of what I had done spread far and wide, and I became a topic of conversation throughout northern California. As a result, I got invitations to games I never knew existed, in California and elsewhere. And in games where I played, people treated me differently. Some scoffed, but most afforded me a subtle respect, or at least an odd sort of notice. At the poker table, players gave me action like never before. As a result of this special treatment, I earned much more than I would have otherwise. The amount of extra profit I netted over the next few years easily surpassed the $7,000 I spent. And on top of that, this story became legendary. People in Santa Cruz talk about it to this day.

The truth is, I considered the possibility of a favorable outcome when I placed that phone call from Las Vegas. I was aware that I could receive a "public relations" boost from giving away that cash. I weighed my risk versus potential long-term benefit. The odds of a good outcome seemed relatively small, or so I thought, but the possible benefit could be significant and long lasting. And I hoped this craziness might be fun in some way; that possibility was worth something, too.

Did my decision pay off in terms of money? Absolutely. But more than that, it paid off handsomely in terms of intangibles. Looking back now, I say it was worth its cost many times over. Sure, it was a risk. It could have turned out to be a foolish action worthy of ridicule. But I made my best guess based on my assessment of the odds. I was not blindly giving away money. I had my best interest in mind, and in this particular case, I won my gamble. I tell you this story not to boast, but to illustrate the mental process of analyzing, in advance, the odds of risk versus benefit.

Honoring exceptions...

I need to make an important point here. Yes, you should incorporate this secret into your thinking, but you should not always act in accordance with the results. In many cases, your smartest move, all things considered, is not to do what your odds would indicate. There are exceptions. Be aware of them.

Let's say you have a life savings of $500,000, and you are ready to retire. I offer you a wager. You put up your $500,000, and I will put up $5,000,000. You roll two dice, and if they come up seven, you win. If they come up anything else, I win. That gives you a one-sixth chance of winning. Should you accept this bet?

Technically, you should. According to your odds of risk versus benefit, this is a good bet. Your odds against winning are 5 to 1, and you are being paid at 10 to 1. In other words, you have a one-sixth (17%) chance of winning, but you are risking only one-tenth (10%) of the amount you could win. So this is a smart wager for you.

Nonetheless, you should turn this bet down. Decline this bet because the most likely outcome is you will lose your life savings. There is a five-sixths (83%) chance you will lose everything you've worked a lifetime to save.

This is a favorable bet for you in the long run. If you were to make this bet one thousand times, you would come out ahead. But placing this bet one time for your life savings is not wise. Bottom line: You cannot afford to lose, and you probably will.

Consider the concept of insurance. Taking out an insurance policy is always a bad bet, from a technical point of view. The policy is designed that way, to be a bad wager for you. Insurance companies know what they are doing. They study the statistics, and they create policies that are wise gambles for them and unwise gambles for everyone else. When you pay $700 per month on a health policy that pays $100,000 should you become hospitalized, that is a bad wager for you because the chance of you landing in the hospital any time soon, according to statistics, is smaller than the ratio of your premium versus payout. Your insurance policy is a wager, and according to its odds of risk versus benefit, it is an unfavorable wager for you. Insurance companies are entitled to make a profit, and they are doing so legally, but from the standpoint of wagering, to put it bluntly, you are being screwed.

So, should you have insurance? Yes, because insurance is an exception. I told you there are exceptions, remember? Well, insurance is one of them. Although, technically, insurance is a bad bet, it is still wise for you to carry certain policies. That is because, should anything catastrophic occur, you are secured by their promise of financial coverage. You cannot afford a $100,000 hospital bill, but you can afford a $700 premium once a month. That is, after all, why people carry insurance. Insurance is a bad bet, but it is a bad bet you should make.

Notice that the first word of this secret is "know." I say, "*Know* your odds of risk versus benefit." I do not say, "*Act* on your odds of risk versus benefit." There are times when your best course of action is to do other than what your odds would indicate. But you should first know what your odds are. Even if you sometimes act contrary to those odds, just knowing what they are makes a huge difference in your thinking, and that knowledge greatly enhances your ability to make wise decisions. When you know your odds of risk versus benefit, you use the laws of probability to guide how your life unfolds.

Tackling your challenges...

Most people go through life not knowing their odds of anything, or even knowing that there *are* odds. You, however, reading this book, realize that everything you do in life is a gamble. With every decision you make, you are placing a wager. The wager may not involve money, but it is a wager nonetheless.

The best way to approach every decision you face is to first know your odds of risk versus benefit. Then consider all other relevant factors. Then, make a decision. Get in the habit of thinking this way all the time. Once you start looking at your decisions in this manner, the process will become second nature to you.

Your goal is to consistently make good decisions. This is analogous to, in poker, making good bets. If you play poker and you consistently make good bets, you will come out ahead. Life functions in the identical way. In life, if you consistently make good decisions, you will succeed. You will win some battles and you will lose some battles, but you will come out ahead over time.

You now have a way to approach your decisions, a way to tackle life's challenges. You have a winning strategy. In everything you do, first know your odds of risk versus benefit, and watch your life improve.

"Play to win, or don't bother. Check friendship at the door. A 'friendly game' is a misnomer."
— Doc Holliday

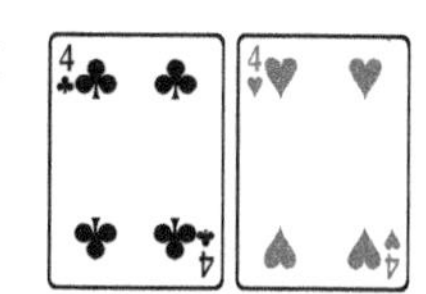

SECRET
NUMBER FOUR

"Fold or raise; don't call."

I hate mediocrity. To me, there is nothing worse than being in the middle. I would rather fail miserably than just get along okay. There are plenty of people who are fine with fitting into the masses. I am not one of them.

Just as I hate mediocrity, I hate calling a bet. When I call, I feel disappointed in myself, as if I let myself down, as if I am seated at a poker table but am unworthy of playing. My heart is beating and my lungs are taking in air, but I am not doing enough with my existence to warrant the blessing of life—that's how I feel when I call.

Yet calling is the main thing most poker players do. That is their primary experience of the game. Call, call, call. They sit there the whole time and never once raise. They fold some hands, but mostly they just call. I bet, they call. I raise, they call. I sneeze, they call. Losers.

You can always pick out the losers at a poker table. I don't mean by seeing whose chips are dwindling. I mean by seeing who is calling all the time. The players that are the calling stations—they are the losers, automatic and predictable. They think they're so hotsy-totsy, but they are weak in the knees.

Do not be one of them. Do not sit down at a poker table if you don't have the courage to compete. The saddest sight in the world is watching some fainthearted player slide into a game and then sit there all night calling. He will lose all his money and never know why. Then he will wimper and whine. Nothing is more pathetic.

Knowing your choices...

I was playing in Amarillo Slim's Super Bowl of Poker tournament in Reno, Nevada. I was on a roll, eliminating players left and right. The way things were going, I had a good shot to win the tournament. My confidence was through the roof, and I felt ready to close things out.

I made it to the final table. There were seven of us left. Howard "Tahoe" Andrew was the chip leader, but I was right behind him. And momentum was on my side.

As seemed likely to happen sooner or later, I got into a hand with Howard. I had A♦ and 10♣; he had A♣ and 3♠. The flop came A♥, J♣, 6♥. We both made Aces, but I had the better kicker. He bet. What did I do? What did I do at that precious moment in time? I called. Horrible move. Next card was the 3♦. He made two pair, won the hand and eliminated me from the tournament.

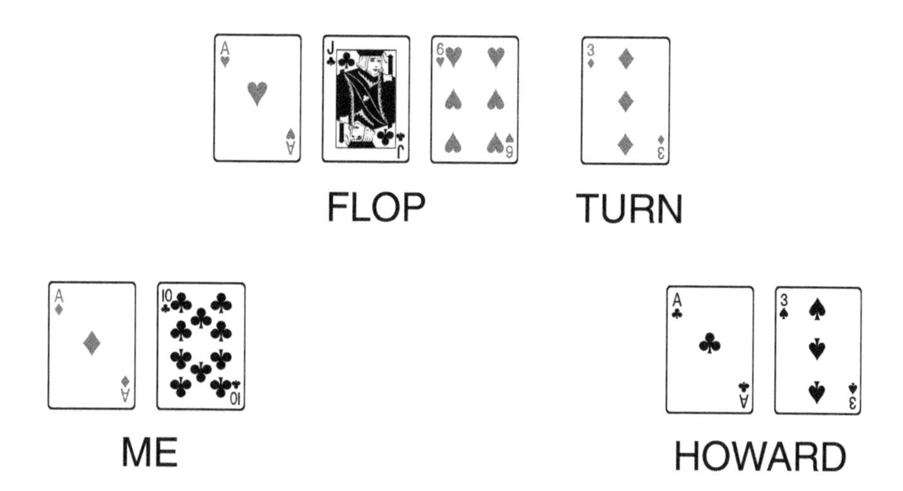

That call was my undoing. I could have folded, and that would have been fine. I could have raised, and that would have been even better. (Howard told me afterward that, had I raised, he would have tossed his hand.) But I called. I let him stick around and catch that 3. I called, and it was a disaster, as it often is. I deserved a kick in the pants.

Here is the secret: Most of the time, when you face an important bet, you should either fold or raise. You can call on occasion, but the less often the better.

Average players do not know this. They think poker is deciding whether or not to call. They think when someone bets into them, they have three choices: call, fold or raise. Although that is true, that is not the best way to think about the decision. Instead, you should think you have only two choices: fold or raise. And oh, by the way, there is a distant third option if you really must, and that is to call. But forget about that.

Only in certain situations is calling acceptable. When a player is all in, raising is not possible, so calling is fine; calling as part of a slow-play strategy is okay; and you should call sometimes to mix up your style. Obviously, you need to call a few bets as a normal part of playing. But when it comes to the big, important bets, as a general rule, you want to be folding or raising, not calling. And when you do call, nobody says you need to like it.

Coming out for blood...

Poker is a game of aggression. If you cannot be aggressive, don't play. You want to be the major force at the table, the force to be reckoned with. You want to be the player everyone fears, the player who inflicts pain.

Poker is not nice. Every moment you sit in a game, play as ferociously as you can. Never, ever, cut anyone slack. Never show mercy. This does not make you a mean person; it makes you a fierce competitor. And if you are not out for victory, what the heck are you doing at a poker table? You can be nice some other time.

The people you play with—it is okay to enjoy and appreciate them. You can have dinner with them. You can go bowling with them. You can loan them money. You can be the greatest chum in the world, but when you sit with them at a poker table, your objective should be to beat them into a quivering pulp.

Without that desire, the dynamic of the game breaks down. In poker, the player who is most aggressive usually wins. Whoever lays out the strongest vibe usually comes out on top. Let that be you. You be that player with the power, that player with the chips, that player everyone is gunning for. Any one hand, you might lose, but over time, you will come out ahead.

Whenever you feel like calling a bet, stop yourself. Consider raising instead. A raise says you are strong. A call says you are weak, indecisive, unsure. Even a fold does not say you are weak; a fold says you are smart. But a call says you barely deserve to be there.

Calling is like delaying your decision. You can't figure out what to do, so you just call and see what happens. A fold or raise requires making that decision now, taking a stand, committing one way or another. A fold or raise makes a statement. A call makes a sigh.

Here is an important fact of poker: In most situations where a call is warranted, a raise is also fine. In other words, few situations exist in which a call is okay but a raise is not. If you should call, then you can raise.

Say you have J♦ and 10♦, and the flop comes K♣, Q♦, 4♦. Your opponent bets into you. He probably has you beat right now, but you have a flush draw and a straight draw. You have a calling hand.

FLOP

YOU

OPPONENT

This situation is common, where you are probably beat but have a great draw. Raise. You could just call, but consider the possibilities. If you raise, he might fold right then. That is good, because you win without a made hand. If he calls, you are in great shape with two cards to go, and if you eventually win the hand, a raise makes you more money in the end. By raising now, you gain power, and you carry more strength into the next betting round. Most players in this situation call, but remember, if you should call, you can raise.

Raising is your finest moment. I am amazed how many players deprive themselves of the experience. Just saying the words is a fulfillment of destiny. “I raise.” What a joy! “I'm all in.” You don't get words more satisfying or empowering than those.

I remember a game in which I was really tearing it up. I was in control of the table. And some great players were there: Seymour Lebowitz, Sam Petrillo and Tommy Hufnagle, all world-class players.

One particular hand, I was dealt 3♣ and 5♥. I raised before the flop. I got reraised, and I raised again. At that point, nobody would put me on a 3-5 off suit. The flop came 3♦, 5♠, 5♣. Needless to say, I went all in. When I got called, the pot grew to over $45,000.

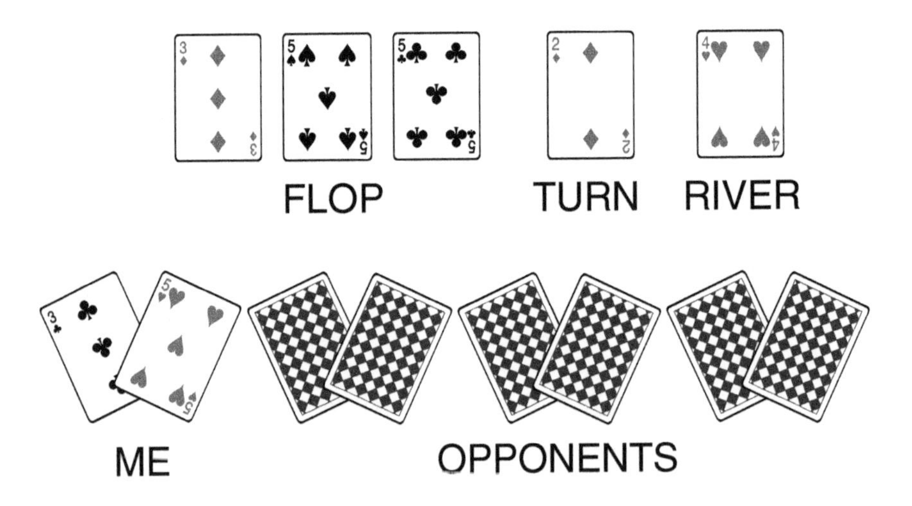

I remember Seymour saying before we turned over our cards, "I hope you're sloshing it around as much as we are." I replied, "I sure am," as I showed my full house. I looked like the master of the universe. Moments like that are what you live for in your poker-playing life. But those moments never come if you're not out there raising. Although I appeared to have supernatural powers, I did not. I simply picked my spot and played aggressively. That's how to play the game of poker. That way, when you connect, everyone pays you off.

Use a combination of folds and raises. The secret is to sit quietly, but when you come out, come out swinging. Come out for blood. Be like a wolf hiding in the shadows, waiting to attack, eager to rip flesh.

One part of this secret involves raising, but don't forget the other part, folding. Folding is important. You should fold most of the time. I cannot emphasize this enough. Fold frequently, and do not feel the lesser for it. Doyle Brunson says, "It's not the hands you play, it's the hands you fold that determine whether or not you'll have a positive bottom line." Laying down your cards is good; it saves you money. Look for reasons to fold, and be glad when you find them.

This advice surprises people. They expect me to encourage raising. Raising is sexy. But folding? Most players see folding as a form of defeat. It is not. Folding is a necessary part of winning. When you fold, you win all that money you didn't lose. And that money is just as sweet as money in the pot. In a real sense, when you fold, you win. And you get to keep playing. Hooray! Recognize folding for what it is, a well-deserved victory. Never regret the hands you fold.

On the flip side, when you don't fold, when you jump into a pot, you should jump in with both barrels blazing. Be fearless. Pick your spots. And when you pick a spot, let 'em have it. Blast in and be heard. Play like that, and you will end up a winner.

Taking chances...

This secret also applies to life. Most of the time, live quietly. Keep to yourself, and wait for your moments. And then, when you decide to make some noise, bust their eardrums.

I know a number of actors in Hollywood. They tell me the key to success in their industry is to "take chances." That's what they call it. When they audition for a part, they try to take chances with the read. They do not want to interpret the character in the obvious way, to read like everyone else. They want to make bold decisions about the character and take risks. They are gambling that the director will like the strong choices they make. They are sticking their necks out, but that is the way to rise above the crowd. To read adequately is like calling a bet. To read in a way that is different, a way that could be great or could be horrible, is like raising a bet.

One of my favorite expressions is "Go for the gusto!" I have no idea who said it first, but I admire the sentiment. Raising a bet is like going for the gusto. When you raise a bet, you announce your courage and commitment. Whether in poker or in life, go for the gusto!

Several years ago, a woman came to me for advice on her struggling health-food business. She was trying to run the company efficiently, yet her revenue continued to decline. I had several talks with this woman, and I discovered that she had an aversion to risk-taking. All her life, her parents had belittled her, and she had developed an unremitting fear of taking chances.

I advised her to gamble and pump some money into her business. I gave her specific recommendations on how to change her advertising and her positioning in the marketplace. She did not like the idea of risking more capital, but she did as I suggested.

Last I heard, her business was doing well and growing every year. When I asked her what made the difference, she replied, "Having the courage to stick my neck out and not be scared of getting it chopped off."

A number of years ago, I consulted for Richard Bertram, the founder and former president of Bertram Yachts. He wanted to hold a meeting, and he asked my advice on what size room he should rent. He was inclined to rent the same size he had always rented, but I advised otherwise. I told him to rent the next size larger.

Several people were seated at the conference table when I told him this, and every one of them disagreed with me. They said they could never draw that many attendees from the region, and renting a larger room would be a waste of money. I argued that renting the bigger space would create the mindset and the energy to produce results. To my way of thinking, renting the same-size space was like calling a bet, doing the ordinary thing. Renting a larger space was like raising a bet, putting more funds at risk and going for greater reward. In this case, I felt the risk was worth taking.

I prevailed. They rented the larger room. Renting that room motivated them to work their butts off publicizing the event. As I predicted, the meeting was a success. They drew more people than they thought possible, and the room was packed. When the time came for their next meeting, they went with an even bigger room. Although renting a room is a minor issue, a valuable lesson can be learned: If you are going to do something, then for cryin' out loud, really do it!

Whatever you do, do it with assertiveness and determination. If you start a new business, have the attitude that you will pulverize all who stand in your way. You will stop at nothing short of total market domination. Do not be content to grind out an adequate income like everyone else. That is like calling a bet. Do not call, raise. Bet everything. Of course, it is perfectly okay not to start your business in the first place. There is no shame in that. That is like folding a hand. You save money and aggravation. But if you decide to take the leap, to put your money into the pot (so to speak), then give it all you've got.

If you want to build a new house, do not settle for something other than what you want. Build the home of your dreams. If you decide not to build a new house, that's fine. But if you decide to go ahead with it, then make it a masterpiece.

If you want to become a professional golfer, do not piddle around in the game. Study and practice every moment you can. Work and work and work, and then work some more. If you decide not to pursue a career in golf, that's A-OK, no crime in that. But if you decide to give it a go, then pour your heart into it. Don't waste time doing it halfway. Do it all the way or not at all.

In life as in poker, you should decline competition (fold) most of the time. Do not fight the majority of potential battles you come upon. Again, this advice might surprise you. You might think I would suggest that you summon the forces of positive thinking and charge headlong into every possible battle. Instead, I say fold most of the time. Select only important challenges in which to commit your time and effort. Do battle rarely, and only when the potential benefit justifies the risk. Be picky about when you engage your precious life energy.

There is no shame in deciding not to do something, because nothing is lost. There is no shame in doing something with all your heart, because if you fail, you can still be proud of your effort. There is shame only in doing something halfway, because if you don't try your best, then you never know whether you might have succeeded otherwise. Failure for lack of sufficient effort is an awful result. You end up with a life of regret.

Bobby Baldwin, who won the World Series of Poker in 1978 and became the CEO of MGM Mirage, put it this way: "The first thing you've got to understand is that there's nothing wrong, nothing sinful, nothing insane about taking reckless chances. Anyone who ever made an invention, fought for justice or climbed a mountain took a chance. The people who risked security the most, the ones who put their stability or their bankrolls on the line—those are the great ones sparkling from cover to cover throughout every history book."

Tony Robbins, perhaps the best-known motivational speaker in the world, said, "If you want to play the game and win, you've got to play 'full out.' You've got to be willing to feel stupid, and you've got to be willing to try things that might not work." Bob Dylan said it with few words: "Go for it, and don't look back."

Living with intensity...

I give you one word: intensity. That is what this secret is about. Live with intensity. If you cannot do something with intensity, then don't do it at all.

Throughout my life, people have often criticized me for being too intense. My tenth-grade English teacher took me aside one day to tell me why she didn't like me. "You're too intense," she said. An ex-girlfriend of mine said the same thing. When she dumped me for a guy at the car wash, she said, "You're too intense." Even my motorcycle buddies had the same comment: "You're too intense." I know these people meant their remark as a criticism, but I have always taken it as a compliment. I figure if I am too intense for most people, then I must be doing something right.

Through intensity, things get done. Do you think the great movers and shakers of this world go about their activities in a casual way? Absolutely not. They pour themselves into everything they do. A forceful attitude makes things happen.

The applied focus of human energy works miracles. Your subconscious mind has the power to transform your efforts into concrete results, but that only happens when you act with intensity. Do not suppress your intensity. Nurture it. Cultivate it. Bring it out.

Earlier in this chapter, I said that if a poker hand is worth a call, then it is worth a raise. The same principle applies to everything in life. If something is worth doing, then it is worth doing with intensity. Do it with every ounce of strength you can muster. Raise the stakes.

And quit calling so much! It is fine to fold, to drop out of life's battles when they do not look promising. Pick your spots. And when you decide to spring into action, raise like there is no tomorrow.

"It is difficult to excel at something you don't truly enjoy."
— Jack Nicklaus

SECRET
NUMBER FIVE

"Have passion! Or do something else."

I am going to tell you a story about me losing. That's right, I lost. I lost decisively, and it was embarrassing.

The story takes place quite a few years ago in Las Vegas. Those days, the Stardust casino was one of the premiere places for high-stakes, no-limit poker. I played there regularly. I noticed another guy who played there, too. He was there nearly every day, at least as much as I was. He and I were two players who consistently made money in those games. His name was Johnny Chan. Johnny won the World Series of Poker two years in a row and was inducted into the Poker Hall of Fame (and appeared in the movie *Rounders*). But this story takes place before all that.

People at the Stardust warned me about Johnny Chan. "He beats everyone heads-up," they told me. ("Heads-up" means only two players.) That got me interested. One day, Johnny and I decided to play each other heads-up. We headed to the Four Queens casino, where we found a table and a dealer. We each put up $10,000.

It was a good match, for a while. He had the lead, then I had the lead. Then he pounced. He cleaned me out. I got up, shook his hand, went back to my room and fell asleep.

You might wonder why I would tell you this, why I would recount a story involving myself that has an unfavorable outcome. Well, we all lose sometimes. I am not ashamed of losing. Charles Schwab said, "I have failed forty-nine percent of the time and succeeded only fifty-one percent of the time." As long as I am ahead overall, I have no reason to hide the times I've lost. I tell you this story because I learned something from the experience. I uncovered an important factor having to do with my loss.

First, let me say that Johnny Chan is an incredible poker player, one of the best. I feel honored to have played against him. That being said, I should not have played him when I did.

In those days, my usual poker-playing pattern was to play one long session, usually 24 to 36 hours, then take a couple of days off to rest and recuperate. Then I would repeat the cycle. When I played Mr. Chan, I was at the end of my playing cycle, after about 36 hours of play. My concentration was off, and I had reached the point where I should have stopped playing. But I wanted this match, so I did not pay attention to that. I can be bullheaded sometimes, and this was one of those times. I wanted to win, but I lacked my usual passion for the game. I lost. Could I beat Johnny Chan now? I don't know. Maybe we'll have a rematch someday.

Bursting with energy...

Poker consists of many decisions, but the biggest decision of all is *when* to play in the first place. When should you get into a game? When should you cash out? Poker books devote a lot of print to these questions.

Most books say you should decide when to play based on preset limits. Some say you should set a limit on your losses, and if you lose that much, stop playing. Some say you should set a limit on your winnings, and if you win that much, stop. Some say you should set a specific time limit, and when you reach that time, quit. Truth is, all these approaches are wrong. They are arbitrary, and they are not what you should consider. The only factor that should determine whether or not you play, at any moment, is your level of passion.

Let me speak about passion. In my experience, passion is the single most determining factor in how a player performs. It is huge. Without passion, a player is merely occupying space at the table. He is receiving cards and placing bets, but he may as well be a computer that is programmed to play. In time, good players will deplete the chips in front of that computer. But with passion, there is a certain glow about the player, as if he were truly alive, bursting with energy, exploding with an unmistakable presence. Money tends to gravitate toward that energy.

When I speak of passion, I am not speaking of a desire to make money or a desire to win. I am referring to one quality: love of the game.

I hope you recognize the feeling I am describing. It is an intense and immediate love of the game—not for the money you can make, not for the fame you can attain, but for the wonderful game of poker itself. I am talking about a love affair: a love for every facet of the game, for its incredible beauty, so beautiful you cannot help but worship its magnificence with every breath you take. You feel gratitude that the game of poker exists, that generations of players have lived and died to perfect this pure treasure, that it is here now and you have the privilege of sitting at a table in the 21st century and partaking in this miracle of competition. You love all the world because poker is part of it.

Most people who play poker do not have that kind of passion. Sure, they sit there trying to win. They may have a thirst for victory, but they do not feel the game coursing through their veins. They do not feel an acute appreciation for the splendor of all that is poker. They appreciate the money or the glory, but not the game itself.

I love poker! There, I said it. When I am feeling that overwhelming love for the game, that wild and unrestrained adoration of everything poker, that is when I should be playing. When I lose that level of excitement, when I cease to feel that crazy love, that is when I should not be playing. It's that simple. This is not about the desire to win or the want to make money; this is about passion, pure unadulterated passion, and nothing else.

Being fully present...

I have discovered a way to gauge my level of passion. I pay attention to how well I am concentrating. If I am concentrating well, if I am able to tune in to the game fully, then my passion is strong.

There comes a time when my concentration slips. There is no mistaking when it happens; I can feel it. It usually happens before 36 hours of continual play. I don't decide ahead of time I will play x-number of hours and then stop. I don't like preset limits. I go until my concentration dies, whenever that is. If that happens at three hours, I quit. If that happens at 36 hours, I quit then. I simply monitor my concentration, and I let that decide how long I play.

Johnny Moss, winner of three World Series of Poker championships and a member of the Poker Hall of Fame, put it this way: "The man with the best concentration will almost always win." I nearly titled this secret "Concentrate." But passion is at the root of concentration. I cannot imagine having passion and not being able to concentrate. Nor can I imagine having the ability to concentrate without passion raging underneath.

The determining factor in when to play poker is not your bankroll or your time schedule; it is your passion. If your passion is strong, then keep playing. Even if you are losing more than usual or playing longer than normal, remain in the game. If you are able to concentrate and you figure to win at that particular table, then you have a good situation working for you. Stay with it. If, however, the excitement has left you, if your level of concentration is down and you are not fully present at the table, get out. Even if you have not played as long as you normally do, stop. Regardless of whether you are winning or losing, or any other factor, head for the door.

Instead of playing poker, do something else. Take a walk, play a computer game or sit and stare at a wall. Do something less dangerous than poker. Clean the cat litter box. Watch television for six hours like a brain-dead zombie—that is preferable to sitting in a poker game when you should not. At least when you turn the television off, you still have some semblance of who you used to be. Besides, the game of poker deserves better than to have a big oaf like you sitting there taking up space, space where another player could be sitting, a player with some passion.

Letting passion decide...

Many times during your journey through life, you face decisions whether to engage in specific competitive encounters. I have the same advice regarding life's battles as I do regarding poker: Let your passion dictate when to compete. Keep in mind that when I speak of passion, I am referring to your level of excitement for the specific activity itself, not for the fame, the money or anything else you might gain as a result of the activity. The following are a few examples to illustrate what I mean.

Let's say you are trying to decide whether to buy some property to develop. The investment could make you a pretty penny if all goes well. What should you do? The answer: Get in touch with your level of passion. There could easily be headaches along the way, and you might need to put a lot of effort into the project. If you feel excitement for the task itself, for improving the property and building on it, not just for the profit you could make, then go ahead and purchase the land. If not, find some other place to invest your time and money.

Let's say you are trying to decide whether to take a second job. You could use the extra cash. Should you do it? The answer: Let your passion decide. You might find you hate the work and the time it requires. You might need more motivation than just the desire for cash. If you feel excitement for the specific job, if you truly enjoy the work involved, then give it a shot. If not, look for another way to improve your finances.

Let's say you are trying to decide whether to write a book. You would love to be an author. Should you start writing? The answer: Check your passion. Writing a book requires dedication and long hours. If you feel excitement for shaping your thoughts into words, and you have something you are dying to tell the world, then sit down and get your ideas on paper. If not, do something else to boost your self-esteem.

Let's say you are trying to decide whether to run a marathon. You would love to share your accomplishment with everyone. Should you sign up? The answer: See what your passion has to say. Training for the event could be a strain, and you may need to push yourself beyond your normal endurance. If you feel excitement for running and making your body perform, not just for the praise of others, then go for it. If not, find some other way to impress your friends.

Let's say you are trying to decide whether to have children. You think starting a family would be marvelous. Should you? The answer: What does your passion say? Raising children is a demanding and all-encompassing vocation. Children are a lifelong commitment. If you feel excitement for loving and nurturing a unique human being, not just for the return love you might get, then leap into this wonderful adventure. If not, seek some other source of fulfillment.

Let's say you are trying to decide whether to sing karaoke. You imagine how cool it would be to belt out your version of a Barry Manilow tune for everyone to ooh and aah. Should you climb on stage? The answer: passion. This could prove to be a disaster if you are out of tune and out of rhythm. If you feel excitement for the act of singing, singing for singing's sake, regardless of what anyone thinks of you, then get up there. If not, stay in your seat and watch the show. Your friends will thank you.

No matter what you attempt to do, if you lack passion, you will fail. If you are a poker pro and you lose your passion for the game, you will lose money. If you are a certified public accountant and you lose your passion for numbers, you will lose clients. If you are a race car driver and you lose your passion for driving, you will lose races. If you are a trapeze artist and you lose your passion for performing, well... it could be a bloody mess. Whatever you are doing, if you lose passion for it, you are well advised to stop and do something else.

Thriving within you...

In poker, one thing that can cause you to lose passion is a "bad beat." A bad beat is defined as a situation where you are likely to win, but something unlikely occurs and you lose. This happens all the time; it is part of the game.

You have two aces, and your opponent has two 4s. The flop comes J♦, A♥, 4♣. Now you have three aces, and he has three 4s. The turn card is 7♦. Now, the only card in the deck that can beat you on the river is the one remaining 4. The chance of you winning this hand is about 98%. You played well, you got your opponent all in, and everything is just the way you want it. Then, the dealer flips over the final card, and it is that dad-blamed 4. You lose. That's a bad beat. It always stings when it happens.

A bad beat can cause you to go on "tilt." Tilt is when you get upset and start playing poorly. Tilt is the same as losing your passion for the game. You don't much like poker right then. When you go on tilt, the smartest thing you can do is get out of the game immediately. Come back after you cool down.

A bad beat can happen in life, too. You might be doing everything perfectly. Every move you make is brilliant. You have every situation just the way you want it, and you are riding on top of the world. Then all of the sudden, out of nowhere, the most unlikely thing happens. Some particular event that almost never occurs actually happens, and it ruins everything. You go bust. (If you play the stock market, you understand what I'm saying.) This sort of experience can put anyone on tilt. If this happens to you, and you feel your excitement fade, take a break. Do not charge back in and attempt to recoup your losses. Get away from the situation at once.

The main consideration is passion. If you feel your passion alive and thriving within you, keep going. If you feel your passion slipping away, get out. If your passion does not return, do something else. Do not go back to what you were doing, or you will get beat up even worse. There are plenty of worthwhile activities available on this lively planet. Surely, you can find something else that excites you.

Following your heart's desire...

Here is a lesson taught in money-making seminars: Do what you should be doing, and the money will follow. This means you should first determine what you like to do. Then do it, and don't worry about making money. If you are doing the right thing, money will come along somehow.

Most people do the opposite. They go out and get some dumb job. Then they try to drum up enthusiasm for that job. Sometimes that works, but more often, it fails. Instead, discover what excites you, and do that. No matter how much of a challenge it presents, go after it. Follow your heart's desire. Don't worry about money, fame or anything else. If you are doing what you should be doing, all else will follow. The problem comes when you are doing something other than what you should be doing, not paying attention to the dictates of your passion. That is when you get in trouble. That is when you go belly-up.

So, stop doing that. Stop being a wuss in life. Pay attention to your passion and have the courage to venture where it leads you. Have the guts to pursue your dreams.

Maybe you think this advice is too idealistic. In the real world, you need to be practical. You need to stay in a dead-end job because people are depending on you. You cannot run around wishing on dreams and have others pay the price for your irresponsibility. Hey, I understand that point of view. Nevertheless, what I am telling you is true. This is how the universe works.

Evaluate what you are doing. If you detect a passion for it, then continue with enthusiasm and determination. If passion is absent, give it up. You are not doing anyone, least of all yourself, any favors by clinging to your self-imposed slavery. Do something else, something for which you feel excitement. For heaven sakes, do not continue on your way without passion, because without passion, you've got nothing.

"Life is always fighting
for survival."
— Mimi Tran

LIFE
(AND POKER)

I do not often lose. No matter what the game, I usually come out on top. I am one of those people everyone hates to see sitting there when they bring out the board games. "Oh, no, not him again... (grumble)." Yeah, that's me.

Why do I usually win? The reason I perform well in competition is no mystery. In fact, it is not even a secret anymore. I just gave away my best secrets. Did you read the preceding five chapters? There's your answer.

In life, your stakes are much greater than they are when playing a board game, or a poker game for that matter. Your stakes *are* your life. And the skill with which you play determines your fate.

Keeping the focus...

In poker, one important fact most players never understand is this: Your goal is to win money, not hands. This is a simple concept, but almost no one gets it. The majority of those who play are constantly trying to win the most hands at the table. They try desperately to take down those tiny pots, and they beam with pride when they scrape a few chips in their direction. Then along comes a big pot. They put lots of money into it, and they lose. Those players lack perspective. No matter how many times they sit there getting smacked around, they never figure out what is wrong.

There is no prize for winning the most hands. The objective in poker is to win the most money. A good player might pass on several small pots, but he is waiting for his moment. Then he wins a monster. Maybe he wins fewer total pots than other players, but he goes home with the most money. That is the player you want to be.

The same principle applies to life. You are not here to win the largest number of minor skirmishes. You are here to win life's best rewards. And life is made up of an assortment of battles, large and small.

Here is a question for you. According to ancient ninja philosophy, when you find yourself in a physical fight, what should be your goal? Almost everyone answers this question "to win." Wrong answer. The correct answer is "to survive." It is better to survive, to lose the fight but come away with only bruises, than to win, to kill the other guy but end up paralyzed from the neck down. Trying to survive is thinking smart, living to fight another day. Trying to win at all costs might impress the crowd gathered to watch, but it is thinking foolishly, ignoring long-term risks. Winning is wonderful, but you win only if you are first able to survive.

Focus on what matters. Engage in battles that make a difference in your life. Do not be a fool, risking life and limb on battles that are of little consequence. Be smart.

Here is another fact of poker most players do not realize: All the poker you play throughout life is one long game. Most players think it is important to win their current playing session. I have seen players stay at a table far longer than they should, trying to get even in that particular game. The truth is, ending up ahead or behind in one session does not matter. What matters is how you end up for your entire experience at poker. It is fine to lose 200 times and win 100 times, if you end up with a profit all told.

This principle also applies to life. Your goal is to come out ahead over time. Do not put undue emphasis on any one competitive contest. Keep your focus on the large picture. Small, insignificant battles do not mean much; large, important battles decide your life's course.

Every experienced poker player has endured countless losses and bad breaks. A good player is not ashamed of losing any one time—as long as he played well. Therein lies the nugget of wisdom. If he played well, but some unlikely occurrence caused him to lose one session, a seasoned player understands that a single event is inconsequential overall. As long as he is playing well, he knows he will come out a winner in the long run.

The same goes for life. If you are competing well, but you lose one particular battle through some weird turn of events, do not freak out. You are still destined to win overall. Get up, dust yourself off and forge ahead.

As you go forth, apply these five secrets. Because life is full of competition, these secrets are perfect. They are exactly what you need. If you are tired of losing, then use them to start winning.

I am not a good loser. Losing makes me sick. If you feel the same way, great. I like that about you. That means you have the necessary drive to win. To heck with being a good looser! Instead, be a good winner!

Looking at victory...

Let's look at specific victories and see how the winner's actions can be viewed from the standpoint of these five secrets. Each of the following victories contains elements of these secrets in action.

On Sunday, June 14, 1998, Michael Jordan hit one of the most amazing shots in the history of NBA basketball. It happened in Game 6 of the championship series, when the Chicago Bulls were in Salt Lake City facing the Utah Jazz.

With less than a minute to play in the game, the score was 86-83 Utah. Jordan received an inbound pass and laid the ball in, trimming Utah's lead to one point. Then the Jazz brought the ball up court and fed it to Karl Malone. As Malone cradled the ball, Jordan swatted it out of his hands for a steal. He then dribbled up court and paused at the top of the key, eyeing his defender, Byron Russell. With only seconds left, Jordan faked a move to the right, then crossed to his left so quickly that Russell fell backwards. Jordan made a jump shot, winning the game 87-86 and giving the Bulls their sixth NBA championship.

In those days, Michael Jordan was so dominant that the one thing no team wanted in the closing seconds of a game was for Jordan to get the ball. Utah players feared, more than anything, that the ball would end up in the hands of Michael Jordan and he would get a shot off. It was easy to determine what the Jazz did not want Jordan to do, so that is exactly what he did.

And he could not have succeeded without focusing on other players. As he stole the ball from Malone, dribbled up court, faked his defender and shot, Jordan was obviously not thinking about himself. His focus was entirely on the players around him. Jordan's final move against Russell was a perfect example of an acute focus on another person.

The shot was also a good percentage play. Jordan shot 15 of 35 from the field that day, including 16 points in the fourth quarter and 8 points in the final two minutes. A shot from his favorite location at the top of the key was a good gamble, especially when the potential benefit was an historic come-from-behind victory for a sixth title. His odds of risk versus benefit made this shot a good bet.

Nothing about this shot was like calling. It was an all-or-nothing, go-for-broke raise. As the ball left Jordan's hands, he was gambling with Chicago's season, taking a risk with one bold move, one trajectory of the basketball. Jordan was raising with all his chips.

Did Michael Jordan play with passion? The answer is obvious. And his passion could not be held down by stomach flu (which he had that day). You can be sure that Michael Jordan did not play that game to secure more money or fame; he played that game because that is where his passion led him. In taking that shot, Jordan was fulfilling his destiny, doing what he was born to do. A person following his passion is a thing of beauty.

That shot will go down in history as quintessential Michael Jordan. When people remember Jordan on the court, they will recall his successes, his incredible victories, not his defeats. Interestingly, he explains his phenomenal lifetime of success this way: "I've missed more than 9,000 shots in my career. I've lost almost 300 games. Twenty-six times, I've been trusted to take the game-winning shot and missed. I've failed over and over and over again in my life. And that is why I succeed."

On November 14, 1994, at the Aladdin Hotel in Las Vegas, Bill Gates, president of Microsoft, delivered a speech that shocked the computer world. It was a presentation entitled "Information at Your Fingertips—In the Year 2005."

Gates talked about how, in ten years hence, we would all have access to a new information superhighway called the Internet. He described "web-type pages," and he said the day would come when people would be able to meet each other in "cyberspace." There would come a day, he suggested when people would shop and bank online. His predictions seemed outlandish at the time, but every one has come to pass.

He also announced that Microsoft would create a web-browser called Internet Explorer. In those days, Netscape owned the browser market, and many industry experts said this move by Microsoft was reckless and would lead to huge losses for the company. Today, Microsoft dominates the browser market and Netscape is all but gone. Bill Gates, with his vision of the future, won his many battles against all competitors.

Back then, the one thing Netscape and its partners were hoping Microsoft would not do was go after the browser market. So, that is exactly what Gates did. And he made this move while paying close attention to other companies and the industry as a whole. He also analyzed his odds of risk versus benefit. There was great risk, but the potential benefit seemed enormous. With his vision of a new and all-pervasive Internet world, Gates reasoned that whoever controlled access to that world would be in a powerful position for many years to come. He wanted that position for Microsoft, and he was prepared to do battle for it.

The move to enter the web-browser market seemed brash and ill-advised back then, much like raising a bet might seem. If Microsoft had wanted to only call a bet, the company could have continued to market its already proven software and let it go at that. Gambling on the browser market, picking a fight with the entrenched market leader, was definitely raising the stakes.

Does Bill Gates have passion? Here is a man who lives and breathes technology. Computers are his driving purpose in life. When he sits in his garage warming up his car, he reads technical papers he posted on his garage wall. That is passion. Gates ended his speech that day saying, "The opportunity here is unbelievable. Looking back, the PC industry has come a long ways. But it's nothing compared to what's going to happen here. I am more excited about this and these possibilities than I ever have been." You can feel the passion when he speaks.

In December of 2012, Denise Stapley, a sex therapist from Cedar Rapids, Iowa, won top prize among 18 competitors in CBS television's *Survivor*. Of course, not everyone has a high opinion of *Survivor;* you might think it is a stupid reality show. Nevertheless, you must admit that it is an example of tough competition and the winner deserves credit for outplaying other contestants.

Many times throughout the contest, Ms. Stapley intentionally did things her opponents did not want her to do. And she was forever watching and studying the other players. Her powers of observation were apparent.

Denise was also aware of her odds of risk versus benefit. Toward the end of the season, the few players remaining felt great concern regarding who should go to the final-three tribal council, whether to take someone well-liked or someone reviled. Denise was masterful in the final episodes as she negotiated with the other players, evaluated various risk factors, and manipulated her way into a position to win.

Denise is a motivator and a huge believer in positive energy. "Life is what you make it, folks," she says. She is not afraid to venture boldly into unknown territory, much like raising a bet. She attributes her victory to her ability to connect deeply with people and gain their trust, in other words, to look outward. And she does not underestimate the importance of passion. In an interview with Entertainment Weekly following her victory, she exclaimed, "Every one of us out there is so passionate about the game!"

Countless examples of victories exist where elements of these five secrets can be found. Playing with intensity, the 2004 Boston Red Sox won the World Series, ending their curse of 86 years. Knowing his odds at every turn, General Colin Powell led the charge to victory in Desert Storm. Paying attention to her audience, Oprah Winfrey climbed to stardom, becoming the first African-American woman billionaire. Frustrating his competition, Tiger Woods won the Masters by 12 strokes, the largest margin of victory ever. Pursuing their dreams, the 1980 US Olympic hockey team took home the gold medal against impossible odds. Raising the stakes, Filmmaker Peter Jackson created the amazing trilogy *The Lord of the Rings*, and the final installment won 11 of 11 Academy Awards for which it was nominated, including Best Picture. Examples such as these inspire us all.

I am not suggesting that these people knew the five secrets as described in this book. (They couldn't have, because I had not yet written the book.) But their victories illustrate elements found within the five secrets. These people were using the identical principles. Look at any account of victory, no matter where you find it, and you will see aspects of these secrets in the winner's actions. I am often asked how one should apply these secrets in real-life situations away from the poker table. Take a look at success stories like these. That is how.

Enjoying the miracles...

Poker is played with money, and many times throughout this book, I talk about winning from a financial standpoint. But please, do not think I am suggesting that life is about money, that making money is the highest purpose of existence. It is not.

There are other realities that have nothing to do with money. Love, sex, health, music, art, prayer—these are important components of life. Money is a small part of your lifetime journey. Do not worry too much about money. Do not drain your valuable life force obsessing about finances.

Let me tell you a story about Jack Straus. Jack won the World Series of Poker in 1982, six years before his untimely death. Jack was one fine human being.

One day, Jack was in tax court. The IRS claimed he owed three million dollars in back taxes. The case being heard before his was a woman who owed $35,000. She was a single mother whose husband had died, and the government was taking her home and possessions. Jack stood up in the back of the courtroom and yelled, "Your honor, stick it on my tab!" Just like that, Jack gave tens of thousands of dollars to a complete stranger.

Was he nuts? Not at all. Did he fail to understand the value of money? He understood just fine. At the poker table, Jack was ruthless. He played aggressively for every dollar. But Jack recognized that there is more to life than money. Compassion and generosity represent a higher value than the accumulation of wealth.

Life is many things to many people. Some people value their lives and the lives of others very little. They demonstrate their lack of character with everything they do. From my observation, these people make poor poker players. They lack the zest for life. They are without the natural sense of excitement that provides the spark for good players. Likewise, they are poor at the game of life. Whatever measure of success they manage to achieve, they lack the ability to appreciate. These are sad folks, indeed.

Then there are people who relish being alive. You see it in their manner. They treasure life and all it has to offer.

Even in adversity, they enjoy the miracles around them. They respect and value everyone's contribution to the fabric of our world. From my observation, these people have qualities that make good poker players. Some of them play and some of them don't, but I believe they all could. In fact, I wish they would.

People sometimes ask why I don't play poker as much as I used to. I stopped playing daily, high-profile poker a number of years ago because I wanted to do other things. Since then, I hosted a daily radio talk program on three local stations and 81 network stations. I wrote two books and three computer games. I deejayed at several nightclubs. I composed and remixed songs. I produced teen dances. I ran a consulting business. I helped create an encounter-group network. I designed websites. I toured Europe. I played baseball. And I raised my son. I still enjoy every moment at the poker table, but I am first a person with varied interests, and second a poker player. Besides, I wanted to stop playing poker full time and apply these secrets to other areas of my life.

Poker has been good to me. It supported me and my family for many years and gave me plenty of memorable moments—like the time I took first place at the California Pacific circuit, the time I won a diamond necklace for a woman in tears and the time I knocked Bobby Baldwin out of a no-limit tournament. More winning days and good moments lie ahead, I am sure. But poker is not the only game in town. I see my life much like the title of this chapter: "Life (and poker)." Notice that "poker" is in parentheses.

Going forth...

Understand the magnitude of what I am giving you. I am giving you five secrets that have the power to transform your life. I have explained these secrets to you fully, holding nothing back. I urge you to take them, go forth into the world and do good things.

I hope you realize how fortunate you are to have come across this book. There are hundreds of books about poker. There are countless books on self-improvement. There are books on positive thinking. There are books for motivation. There are books for inspiration. There are books with pep talks for success. But no one has written a book anything like this one. After hundreds of years of poker on this globe, no one has taken the valuable lessons within the game and applied them to life. Until now.

The focus of this book is not poker. The focus is the secrets—which happen to come from poker. The secrets work flawlessly at the poker table. And because life is like poker in a fundamental way, these same secrets work when applied to life. What a bonanza!

I have revealed to you the five greatest secrets of poker and life. I have shown you how to win at whatever you do. I have kept my part of the bargain. The rest is up to you.

And I do mean *you*. You are God's precious creation here on this planet. You are the product of unbounded consciousness pulsing through the universe. Maybe you've forgotten who you are. Nonetheless, you are entitled to a healthy share of the world's bounty. You deserve success. You deserve happiness. You deserve everything wonderful life has to offer. You do. And these five secrets will empower you to claim your destiny.

Use these secrets, and great things will happen. You will become a winner. You will conquer all who oppose you. You will triumph at life. And the world will lie down before you. Everything you want is out there. Now, go get it.

afterword

It was a cool autumn day. I found myself in rural Oregon, playing poker. The guy seated across from me was trying to impress everyone. He was a boisterous sort, said he worked in a lumberyard. I sat patiently a long time. I like to pick my spots.

My moment came. The lumberman studied his two cards and bet. I sensed weakness on his part, so I raised. He called.

The flop came Q♥, 8♥, 6♠. He bet. I raised. He called. The next card was 4♣. He checked. I moved all in.

He glared at me. He leaned back in his chair, took off his cap and rubbed his head. He glared some more. He sent a dirty look to everyone at the table. He put his cap back on. He asked the dealer what time it was. He fiddled with something on his belt. He moved forward, put his elbows on the table and stared straight at me. He laughed. Then he tossed his cards. As he did, he bellowed in my direction, “Man, you’re awful damn lucky catching them good cards.”

I decided to show my hand. I turned over a 7-2 off suit, the worst possible hand in Texas Hold 'em. With that, the guy got up, cashed in his chips and left.

I am reminded of something Robert Louis Stevenson said: "Life is not just a matter of holding good cards, but sometimes of playing a poor hand well."

faq
frequently asked questions

Over the years, I have been asked certain questions frequently. Here is how I answer them.

Q... I realize poker is popular these days, but that doesn't make it right. You paint gambling as so wonderful, but it is evil. It is based on greed and trying to get something for nothing, so gambling is a sin. What do you say about that?

A... I say you need to open your eyes and look at the world around you. Whether you like it or not, gambling (meaning risk-taking, in the broad sense) is everywhere. Gambling has long endured a negative portrayal in our society. That's a bum rap. Rather than labeling gambling evil, you would do well to recognize it as an inherent and necessary part of living. Understand the principles involved, use them well and you will benefit enormously.

Q... You are encouraging people to gamble, right?

A... Let's be clear what we mean by "gamble." You probably mean buying lottery tickets and placing bets at a casino. I do not encourage you to gamble in those ways because the house odds are against you, making your bets unwise. What I mean by gambling is the general attribute of life whereby everything you do is a form of risk-taking. In that sense, yes, I encourage you to learn how to gamble wisely to win the many challenges you face in life.

Q... Gambling addiction is a serious problem. Don't you owe an apology to those with gambling difficulties?

A... I realize some people struggle with addiction. People are addicted to food, sex, television and a million other things. But that does not make those things bad. The same goes for gambling. Some people are addicted to gambling. But I do not owe them an apology, any more than the neighborhood bakery owes an apology to those with eating disorders.

Q... I have never played poker. I don't even like poker. Can I still use these secrets?

A... Absolutely. You do not need to understand anything about poker. You need only to understand how to apply these secrets to life. Forget that these secrets come from poker. Ignore all poker discussions in this book. Focus only on the essence of the secrets, and get them into your life.

Q... You say life is like poker. But I don't like how that sounds. Why do you say that?

A... Because it is true. You may not want to hear it, but poker and life both function according to the same immutable laws of the universe. Both consist of a constant stream of decisions, and in life as in poker, success is determined by how well you handle those decisions. The secrets in this book apply equally to poker and life.

Q... Poker is more complex than just your secrets. In high-level play, advanced strategies are involved. Aren't you simplifying how to play poker?

A... Yes, but this book is not primarily about poker. There are plenty of good books that discuss the intricacies of poker, so if you want an advanced poker lesson, read one of those. This book takes the most fundamental and far-reaching secrets of poker and brings them into life. This book is really about life.

Q... Do these secrets work with Internet poker?

A... Many people around the world enjoy online poker. Although the experience of online poker is somewhat different than poker in person, yes these secrets can be used on the Internet. The first two secrets are trickier to implement online, but if you apply them correctly, they work.

Q... Do you play Omaha or 7-card stud?

A... Yes, I play whatever is being dealt. Some players prefer these games. I don't. My favorite game is no-limit Hold 'em. Given the choice, I'll pick that game any day.

Q... I have horrible luck. Am I doomed?

A... Absolutely not. And you don't have horrible luck. It might interest you to know—and this is a documented fact—most professional poker players consider themselves unlucky.

This is the opposite of what you might expect. Successful players often feel they need to play better than other players just to offset their terrible luck. Maybe you feel the same way regarding your life as a whole. The truth is, over an extended period of time, you have no better or worse luck than anyone else. It might seem that you do, but that is an illusion. You tend to remember bad breaks and forget good breaks. Over time, luck balances out, and the law of averages reigns supreme. Make good decisions and don't worry about luck. Do that, and you will come out ahead.

Q... You seem to be critical of things like meditation and self-improvement. How come?

A... I am not criticizing those things. I am actually a proponent of meditative and introspective practices. Self-improvement has its place, and many people derive immense benefit from it. But when it comes to facing life's challenges, to prevailing over specific adversaries, to winning important competitions, in my experience, nothing is as effective as a sound strategy that is known to produce targeted results. These five secrets give you that strategy, if you want it.

Q... Cooperation is better than competition. Why do you slam cooperation?

A... It is not a question of one being better than the other. Both cooperation and competition have their places. When it comes to raising children, for example, you should not enter into competition with your spouse. In that context, cooperation is essential. But there are situations where competition is unavoidable. In fact, competition is the normal way of the world. It is everywhere. You are well advised to learn how to compete and win.

Q... Doing what my opponent doesn't want me to do is great, but what if I can't figure out what that is?

A... Making that determination is, of course, a critical part of this secret. Employ every means at your disposal to figure out what your opponent doesn't want you to do. If you fail to come up with that information, then make a decision some other way. But take heart: Through practice, you will get better at doing this.

Q... How do I counter this secret if someone is using it against me? In other words, if my opponent knows this secret and is trying to determine what *I* don't want *him* to do, how do I prevent that?

A... Almost nobody knows this secret, so you are not likely to encounter someone using it against you. But, if you do, your only option is to try to clear your mind and arrive at a mental state free of all desires. I must tell you, however, that you will probably fail at this Zen-like endeavor, and even if you succeed, your opponent might still pick up an indication of your thoughts. The truth is, if someone is using this secret on you, you are in trouble. You cannot avoid having some desires during competition, and a skilled opponent could deduce what they are. This secret is too powerful to be foiled. So, my advice is: Use it yourself. In other words, make sure you use it first, before anyone can use it on you.

Q... You say look outward. But if I pay attention to everyone else and not myself, won't I neglect my needs and make decisions that are not in my best interest?

A... No, that's not possible. No matter how much attention you pay others, your inner being will not lose sight of your deep-seated desire to win. Do not worry about going too far to the other extreme and acting against your own best interest. It won't happen.

Q... You say everything comes to us from other people. You say we don't grow our own food. Well, *we* do! We have a garden. What about that?

A... Where did you get the seeds? Where did you get the fertilizer? Where did you get the land? What about the tools you used to till the soil—did you build a steel mill and forge the steel for those tools?

Q... Calculating the odds of risk versus benefit is too complicated. Who the heck wants to turn decisions into a complex analytic ordeal?

A... You misunderstand. At the poker table, it is possible to perform statistical and numerical calculations. But when it comes to decisions in life, that is not the case. The goal of this secret is to make your decision-making process easier, not harder. Knowing your odds of risk versus benefit is a way of thinking, a way of approaching your decisions. That's all it is. Keep it simple. You'll get the hang of it.

Q... Getting married is not a gamble if both people love each other and are committed to each other. Why do you have such a cynical view of everything?

A... If you don't see that there is an element of risk-taking in getting married (as there is in everything you do), then close this book right now. Go live a little, and come back after you've done so.

Q... What is wrong with being like most people? What is wrong with fitting in?

A... Nothing, if that is what you want. If you are satisfied with an "ordinary" life, great. I wish you happiness. This book is intended for those who want more, those who feel a nagging sense of dissatisfaction with their lives. If that describes you, then learn these secrets. I am giving you a way to excel.

Q... You say I should fold a lot. Don't you realize how hard that is? I don't like folding.

A... I know. You want action. You want to be in there throwing your chips around. You came to play, not to fold all the time. Folding is no fun. That's why you need patience and discipline. That's why only a fraction of poker players succeed, because it's hard to fold. Calling, on the other hand, is easy. Any moron can do it. You toss in a few chips, and you get to stay in the hand. But heed my words: If your goal is to win, you must take the difficult path. You must fold most of the time. In poker and in life, knowing when to fold is a requirement for success. It's how you rise above the crowd. Maybe that sounds counterintuitive, but it's true. Accept it.

Q... Sometimes, calling a poker bet is the right move. You shouldn't always fold or raise, should you?

A... True, calling is acceptable in certain situations. If a player is all in, for example, raising is not possible, so calling is okay. Sometimes you might call as part of a larger strategy, such as setting someone up for a big bet and then calling them. The point is, as a general rule, when a significant bet comes along, you want to be folding or raising, not calling. In life, the same principle applies. When a significant matter lies before you, either decline to get involved or attack it with all you've got. Don't waffle around and try halfheartedly.

Q... You speak of passion. But can't passion lead me down a wrong path? Can't I be passionate about something detrimental to myself or others?

A... Of course. That is where discernment comes in. You should not always do everything you are passionate about, but you should make sure whatever you decide to do meets the requirement for passion. In other words, do not necessarily do all things for which you have passion (you may not have time), but be certain you have passion for all things you do. This is an important distinction. And if you are contemplating a course of action but do not feel passion, do something else.

Q... Can't I succeed without passion? Aren't some people successful in life without being passionate?

A... No. There are people who inherit their daddy's business and live in luxury, but that does not fit my definition of success. Success comes from achievement. And believe me, nobody achieves anything worthwhile without passion driving them. Passion is necessary. That is how the world works.

Q... You say if I don't have passion, I shouldn't do things. It's not good to sit around and do nothing, is it?

A... Read the wording of that secret again. I don't say lay around and vegetate. I say *"do something else!"* To succeed, you must engage in productive activity. Find something you like to do, then get off your backside and do it! Just make sure you feel passion for whatever it is.

Q... Don't your fourth and fifth secrets say the pretty much the same thing?

A... No, they are different. Secret number four says "Raise or Fold." It deals with how to play effectively once you are engaged in competition. Secret number five says "Have Passion!" It deals with when to compete in the first place. Secret number four is about living with intensity. Secret number five is about gauging your passion and acting accordingly.

Q... You say people should change jobs if they don't like their work. Don't you think that's irresponsible?

A... No, I don't. If you want a meaningful life, that is how you must act. You will never live fully struggling in a career you hate. I will not back down on this point. You must feel passion for what you do. No compromise. Sure, you can get by for decades in the wrong career and still exist (sort of), but that is not fulfilling your destiny. If these words leave you feeling discontent, I am glad. Maybe they will motivate you to reach for your dreams. Do not settle for less than the life you want.

Q... You say life is a game. I've got news for you, there's nothing playful about life. It is a struggle from beginning to end. Do you think it's all fun and games?

A... I've got news for *you*. Life is what you make of it. Do you think you were put on this earth only to toil and suffer and then die in misery? No way! If you believe that, you are mistaken. You have a unique purpose, and you can achieve great things. Yes, there will be difficult times, times of blood, sweat and tears, but you carry within you the potential for a life overflowing with blessing and reward. Approach your problems in a more game-like fashion. Allow yourself to experience the goodness around you. Drop your bitterness, and start winning. Enjoy the bounty of our world.

Q... Your secrets sound good, but success comes from hard work, not a bunch of hocus-pocus. Don't you agree?

A... Hard work and dedication are essential elements of success, but you must also have an effective strategy with which to apply your hard work, otherwise you are spinning your wheels and laboring without results. Look at the millions of people working hard every day and getting nowhere. Obviously, hard work is not the only requirement for success. You also need the right plan of action. Do not confuse the secrets in this book with hocus-pocus. These secrets have a proven track record at the poker table—and in life. From the tone of your question, I sense an attitude of defeatism. If you feel condemned to a life of failure, you need to snap out of that nonsense. The truth is, you deserve the greatest of success and happiness. You have a rightful claim to every bit of joy and celebration the world has to offer. Please, do not close your mind to what these secrets can do for you.

Q... Why reveal these secrets? What's the point?

A... People tell me that these secrets have changed their lives. They tell me I should commit this information to a book, that instead of just talking on my radio program, ranting in my poker classes and preaching to my business clients, I should, once and for all, share these priceless secrets with the world. I agree. I wrote this book so you can learn these five secrets and use them. This book is for you—you with the courage to bring these secrets into your life. For you, I have the highest regard. You will benefit greatly. You will embark on a new life, a life in harmony with your ambitions. You will find success and fulfillment. I know you will. I have faith in you.

appendix a

THE FIVE SECRETS

SECRET NUMBER ONE

"Determine what they *don't* want you to do, then do that."

SECRET NUMBER TWO

"Look Outward."

SECRET NUMBER THREE

"Know your odds of risk versus benefit."

SECRET NUMBER FOUR

"Fold or raise; don't call."

SECRET NUMBER FIVE

"Have passion! Or do something else."

Secret Number One...
"Your opponent is thinking something. He is not blank in the head. He is considering your possible moves, and there is *something* he hopes you do not do. Find out what that is. Go after one piece of information: what he does not want you to do. If you can determine that, you are golden."

Secret Number Two...
"Competition is the time to acquire knowledge of your opponent, and the way to do that is to look outside yourself. These days, with everyone preaching the value of looking inward, I want to offer a little balance. Allow me to strike a bell for the wisdom of looking outward."

Secret Number Three...
"You should first know what your odds are. Even if you sometimes act contrary to those odds, just knowing what they are makes a huge difference in your thinking, and that knowledge greatly enhances your ability to make wise decisions. When you know your odds of risk versus benefit, you use the laws of probability to guide how your life unfolds."

Secret Number Four...
"If a poker hand is worth a call, then it is worth a raise. The same principle applies to life. If something is worth doing, then do it with every ounce of strength you can muster. And quit calling so much! It is fine to fold, to drop out of life's battles. Pick your spots. And when you decide to spring into action, raise like there is no tomorrow."

Secret Number Five...
"Stop being a wuss in life. Pay attention to your passion and have the courage to venture where it leads. Have the guts to follow your dreams. Do not continue on your way without passion, because without passion, you've got nothing."

appendix b

RANK OF POKER HANDS

STRAIGHT FLUSH: five cards in a row suited

FOUR OF A KIND: four matching cards

FULL HOUSE: a three of a kind and a pair

FLUSH: five cards of the same suit

STRAIGHT: five cards in a row

THREE OF A KIND: three matching cards

TWO PAIRS: two pairs of matching cards

ONE PAIR: two matching cards

HIGH CARD: highest single card

The following are odds of being dealt these specific poker hands from five cards selected at random from a 52-card deck. The figures express the probability of that hand *or better*.

Straight Flush: 0.0015 % — 64,973 to 1

Four of a Kind: 0.03% — 3,913 to 1

Full House: 0.17% — 589 to 1

Flush: 0.37% — 272 to 1

Straight: 0.76% — 131 to 1

Three of a Kind: 2.87% — 33.8 to 1

Two-Pair: 7.63% — 12.1 to 1

One Pair: 49.88% — 1 to 1

Of course, you do not need to know these odds in order to benefit from this book, since a knowledge of poker probabilities is not required to apply these secrets to your life. But I thought you might find these figures interesting, particularly as you notice the relative rarity of the higher-ranked hands.

appendix c

GLOSSARY OF TERMS

ALL-IN: A bet consisting of all of a player's chips, leaving no other chips on the table for that player that hand.

BAD BEAT: To lose a hand due to an unlikely occurrence.

BET: Adding a wager in chips to the pot. All other players must match this bet to stay in the hand.

BLIND: A forced bet. Also, a player in early position.

BUTTON: A marker that signifies the player who is in last position for that hand, the dealer.

CALL: Matching a previous bet in order to stay in a hand.

CALLING COLD: Calling a bet and raise all at once.

CASE CARD: A single card in the deck that makes a hand.

CHECK: The same as pass: passing the option to bet to the next player in turn. Folding if a bet is required.

DRAW: Playing a hand while hoping that cards yet to come will make the hand, such as a flush or straight draw.

DRAWING DEAD: Drawing to a hand that, even if made, will still lose.

FLOP: The first three community cards in Hold 'em.

FOLD: To toss one's cards and give up on the hand.

HOLD 'EM: The specific game of poker: Texas Hold 'em.

HOLE CARDS: The two cards dealt face down.

MADE HAND: A hand of cards that is complete and requires no further draw.

NUTS: A hand that cannot be beaten during the hand.

OVER CARD: Any card in a player's hand that is higher than any card among the community cards.

OVER PAIR: A hand that contains a pair of cards higher than any card among the community cards.

POSITION: The player's location within the order of turns for that particular hand.

POT: The central holding area for bets. The total amount bet by all players and eventually won on the hand.

RAISE: Adding to the previous bet to increase the amount wagered. All other players must match the original bet and the raise to stay in the hand.

RIVER: The fifth community card in Hold 'em.

TURN: The fourth community card in Hold 'em.

SNAPPED OFF: To lose a hand badly due to foolish or overly aggressive play.

TELL: A mannerism that reveals a player's hand.

TILT: To play poorly, erratically or desperately due to frustration or emotional upset.

TOP PAIR: A hand that has paired the highest card of the community cards.

WIRED PAIR: A pair made up of the two hole cards.

bibliography

Poker...

Brunson, Doyle. *Doyle Brunson's Super System II*. Cardoza, 2012, 2005. amazon.com/dp/B007E3FA56

Caro, Mike. *Bobby Baldwin's Winning Poker*. Cardoza, 2004. amazon.com/dp/1580421296

Sklansky, David. *The Theory of Poker*. Two Plus Two, 2011, 1999, 1994. amazon.com/dp/1880685000

Chan, Johnny. *Play Poker Like Johnny Chan*. Top Player, 2005. amazon.com/dp/1933074485

Vorhaus, John. *Killer Poker Hold 'em Handbook*. Lyle Suart, 2004. amazon.com/dp/0818406410

Hellmuth, Phil. *Play Poker Like the Pros*. Collins, 2009, 2003. amazon.com/dp/B000FC1Q5Q

Feeney, John, Ph.D. *Inside the Poker Mind: Essays on Hold 'em and General Poker Concepts*. Two Plus Two, 2010, 2000. amazon.com/dp/B003TXSRKK

Caro, Mike. *Caro's Book of Poker Tells*. Cardoza, 2011, 2003. amazon.com/dp/B006305OHA

Malmuth, Mason. *Fundamentals of Poker*. Two Plus Two, 2000. amazon.com/dp/1880685248

Gordon, Phil. Poker: *The Real Deal*. Simon Spotlight, 2004. amazon.com/dp/B000FC2JIE

Brunson, Doyle. *Poker Wisdom of a Champion*. Cardoza, 2003. amazon.com/dp/1580421199

McEvoy, Tom and T.J. Cloutier. *Championship No Limit & Pot Limit Hold 'em*. Cardoza, 2011. 2004. amazon.com/dp/B0062M60AO

Warren, Ken. *The Big Book of Poker*. Cardoza, 2011, 2004. amazon.com/dp/158042113X

Schoonmaker, Alan N., Ph.D. *The Psychology of Poker*. Two Plus Two, 2000. amazon.com/dp/B002Z13PA4

McKenna, James A. *Beyond Tells: Power Poker Psychology*. Lyle Stuart, 2007. amazon.com/dp/B008SLEU90

Fox, Russell & Scott T. Harker. *Mastering No-Limit Hold 'em*. Conjelco, 2005. amazon.com/dp/1886070210

Greenstein, Barry. *Ace on the River: An Advanced Poker Guide*. Last Knight Publishing, 2005. amazon.com/dp/0972044221

Esfandiari, Antonio. *World Poker Tour: In the Money*. Collins, 2006. amazon.com/dp/B003H4RD1U

Harrington, Dan. *Harrington on Cash Games*. Two Plus Two, 2008. amazon.com/dp/B007GJ7J52

Reagan, Brad and Michael Kaplan. *Aces and Kings: Inside Stories and Million-Dollar Strategies*. Wenner Books, 2005. amazon.com/dp/B003H4RD1U

David Apostolico, *Poker and the Art of War*. Lyle Stuart, 2005. amazon.com/dp/081840647X

Sklansky, David. *Hold 'em Poker*. Two Plus Two, 1996. amazon.com/dp/B006OWKLVG

Bellin, Andy. *Poker Nation*. Perennial, 2009, 2002. amazon.com/dp/B000FCK3CI

Life...

Nixon, Richard G. *Lazy Man's Way to Riches*. Penguin, 1995, 1973. amazon.com/dp/1884337228

Seligman, Martin E.P., Ph.D. *Learned Optimism*. Pocket, 2011, 1990. amazon.com/dp/B005DB6S7K

Malcolm Gladwell, *Blink*. Little Brown, 2007. amazon.com/dp/B000PAAH3K

Peale, Norman Vincent. *The Power of Positive Thinking*. Fawcett Crest, 2003, 1952. amazon.com/dp/B000FC0SXM

Hill, Napoleon. *Think and Grow Rich*. Fawcett Crest. 2012, 1960, 1938. amazon.com/dp/B009VKWBF2/

Michael Jordan. *Driven from Within*. Atria Books, 2005. http:/ amazon.com/dp/B001D201DK

Steve Cohen. *Win the Crowd*. Harper Collins, 2009. amazon.com/dp/B000N2HD3W

Leonard, Jim. *The Skill of Happiness*. Three Blue Herons, 2012, 1996. amazon.com/dp/B007UPEYAA

Covey, Stephen R. *The Seven Habits of Highly Effective People*. Free Press/Simon & Schuster, 2009, 1990. amazon.com/dp/ B000WJVK26

George S. Clason. *The Richest Man in Babylon*. Signet, 2007, 2001. amazon.com/dp/B000ZH1GEC

Machowicz, Richard. *Unleash the Warrior Within*. Marlowe, 2011, 2002. amazon.com/dp/0738215686

Ursiny, Tim Ph.D. *The Confidence Plan*. Sourcebooks, 2005. amazon.com/dp/1402203497

Johnson, Spencer. *Who Moved My Cheese?* G.P. Putnam, 1998. amazon.com/dp/B004CR6AM4

Bernard Bill. *Life is Not Fair... and everything else they forgot to teach you in school*. Sourcebooks, 2004. amazon.com/dp/ B003L203LA

Robbins, Anthony. *Awaken the Giant Within*. Fireside, 2007, 1991. amazon.com/dp/B001EM101Q

Keoghan, Phil. *No Opportunity Wasted: Creating a List for Life*. Rodale Books, 2004, 1996. http://www.amazon.com/dp/ 0132638495

Hyrum W. Smith. *What Matters Most: The Power of Living Your Values*. Simon & Schuster, 2001. amazon.com/dp/0684872579

Zig Ziglar. *Over the Top*. Nelson Books, 1997. amazon.com/dp/B002GJU5Q2

Keoghan, Phil. *No Opportunity Wasted: Creating a List for Life*. Rodale Books, 2006, 2004. amazon.com/dp/B004GGUGQC

Ringer, Robert. *Action!: Nothing Happens Until Something Moves*. M. Evans and Company, Inc., 2004. amazon.com/dp/B004BLIP56

Maxwell Matlz and Bobbe Sommer. *Psycho-Cybernetics*. Prentice Hall Art, 2000, 1996. amazon.com/dp/0132638495

Sam Horn. *What's Holding You Back?* St. Martin's Griffin, 2000. amazon.com/dp/0312254407

Campbell, Susan, Ph.D. *Getting Real*. HJ Kramer, 2001. amazon.com/dp/B002L2GK5O

Keyes, Ken. *Handbook to Higher Consciousness*. LoveLine, 1993, 1975. amazon.com/dp/0960068880

Bernie Siegel, MD. *Prescriptions for Living*. Harper, 2011, 1998. amazon.com/dp/B004V52B16

Cameron, Julia, *Walking in this World*. Tarcher Penguin, 2003. amazon.com/dp/1585422614

Jim Loehr and Tony Schwartz. *The Power of Full Engagement*. Free Press, 2003. amazon.com/dp/B000FC0SWS

Jack Canfield and Janet Switzer. *The Success Principles.* HarperResource, 2009, 2005. amazon.com/dp/B000FC2OHA

Thomas J. Stanley. *Millionaire Mind.* Andrews McMeel, 2001. amazon.com/dp/B004EPYWM4

Barbara Sher. *Live the Life You Love.* Dell, 1997. amazon.com/dp/0440507561

Dominguez, Joe, and Vicki Robin. *Your Money or Your Life.* Penguin, 2008, 1992. amazon.com/dp/B0052MD8VO

Dyer, Wayne Dr. *You'll See It When You Believe It.* Avon, 2009, 1989. amazon.com/dp/B0015KGX14

Wilber, Ken, ed. *The Holographic Paradigm.* Shambhala, 1982. amazon.com/dp/0394712374

about the author

Victor Boc's life stands as a testament to the secrets in this book. For example, Victor has been...

- A world-class professional poker player. Victor has won numerous tournaments and competed in the World Series of Poker. He has appeared on national television, been written up in poker publications, managed a poker cardroom and taught poker at a junior college. He has supported his family (and others) for many years playing poker.

- A top-rated radio personality. Victor has hosted programs in cities like Cleveland, Boston, San Francisco, and Portland, as well as a national show in 81 cities across the United States on the Talk America Radio Network. His awards include a place among "The Most Important Talk Show Hosts in America" and Associated Press Awards for "Best Commentary" and "Best Talk Host."

- A best-selling author. Victor's book, "How to Solve All Your Money Problems Forever," has sold more than 200,000 copies worldwide. Through articles, seminars and speaking engagements, he has helped thousands, from all walks of life, achieve financial success. (The book is available at Amazon: flowofmoney.com/ab.)

- A popular nightclub deejay and entertainer. Victor has performed regularly to sellout crowds. His energy has turned several clubs into lucrative businesses.
- A highly-respected business consultant. Specializing in advertising, design and editing, Victor has guided a number of successful enterprises.

These days, in addition to writing, Victor conducts seminars, performs as an electronic deejay, produces entertainment events, consults businesses, designs websites—and plays poker. Living in the beautiful state of Oregon, he devotes a great deal of time to hiking and romping outdoors. And he continually creates fun projects with his son. Victor's achievements do not fit into a narrow category. He is not an easy guy on which to pin a label.

Victor Boc, on the air at KPAM Radio, 860 AM, in Portland, Oregon

VICTOR'S HUMBLE REQUEST

Regarding the matter of customer reviews on Amazon.com... I love them! Not only do they brighten my life, but they serve as valuable reader feedback. I can't get enough of them.

So... I humbly request that you write me one. Please?

If I were a waiter, serving you dinner, you might leave me a tip. Of course, you can't tip me for my book (nor should you), but a review on Amazon is the closest thing to a tip. If you found anything of value in what I wrote, or have any desire to show appreciation, or "tip" me, you have the perfect way to do so. Write a review on Amazon. Anyone can do it, and it's easy. And it means the world to me.

Write your review here:
fivegreatestsecrets.com/ab

This link will send you to Amazon.com. Scroll down the Amazon page until you see the "Customer Reviews" section, and click the button to write a review. There you can express your thoughts, whatever they are.

If you write a review, send me an email message (at victorboc@outlook.com) and tell me which review is yours. I'd like to say thank you.

Even if you don't write a review, I'd still love to hear from you. Tell me your adventures with these secrets or any aspect of your life you want to share. If you absorbed my book, I now take personal interest in you—and your success. Please feel free to write anytime, for any reason.

CONTACT VICTOR

Email — Victor Boc
victorboc@outlook.com

Personal Website — Victor Boc
victorboc.com

Website — This Book
fivegreatestsecrets.com

Amazon Page — Victor Boc
fivegreatestsecrets.com/aa

Amazon Page — This Book
fivegreatestsecrets.com/ab

ALSO BY VICTOR BOC

How to Solve All Your Money Problems Forever
Creating a Positive Flow of Money Into your Life
flowofmoney.com/ab
flowofomoney.com

Just Living and Reproducing
justlivingandreproducing.com/ab
justlivingandreproducing.com

Money Talks

Beyond Your Wildest Dreams

Georgia Bear Can't Dance

index

"It used to not be cool to be a poker player. Now it's cool to be a poker player." — Antonio Esfandieri

"Poker became the national card game of the United States because it suits the American temperament. It is a game for the individual. Each player is on his own, the master of his fate."
— Albert H. Moorhead

"Gambling is a principle inherent in nature."
— Edmund Burke

"It can be argued that man's instinct to gamble is the only reason he's not a monkey up in trees." — Mario Puzo

"Poker is a lot like sex, everyone thinks they are the best, but most have no clue what they are doing." — Dutch Boyd

"Limit poker is a science, but no-limit is an art. In limit, you are shooting at a target. In no-limit that target comes alive and shoots back at you." — Crandall Addington

"Luck is the residue of design. The more prepared you are, the more you study your game, the luckier you become."
— Andy Glazer

"You are rewarded for correct play in the long run; in the short run, anything can happen." — Tom McEvoy

"Nobody is always a winner, and anybody who says he is, is either a liar or doesn't play poker." — Amarillo Slim Preston

"If you can't spot the sucker in the first half hour at the table, then it's you." — Anonymous

"Don't let adverse facts get in the way of a good decision."
— General Colin Powell

"Guessing has never been widely acclaimed as a good gambling strategy." — Dr. G.

"Yeah, well, sometimes nothin' can be a really cool hand."
— Cool Hand Luke

This book is intended to provide information regarding the subject covered. It is sold with the understanding that the author is not engaged in legal or professional services. If such services are desired, a competent professional should be sought. The purpose of this book is to inform and entertain. The author and publisher assume no liability, direct or indirect, resulting from the use or misuse of this information. In no case, regardless of the form of claim, shall liability exceed the cost of book replacement or refund.

THE FIVE GREATEST SECRETS OF POKER AND LIFE

How To Win At Whatever You Do

Victor Boc

2013

CPSIA information can be obtained
at www.ICGtesting.com
Printed in the USA
LVHW092334121218
600290LV00001B/96/P